IN HIS NAME

A STUDY OF THE ABSOLUTE

Other Writings by Lillian DeWaters

All Things Are Yours ✦ The Atomic Age
The Christ Within ✦ The Finished Kingdom
Gems ✦ God Is All
The Great Answer ✦ Greater Works
I Am That I Am ✦ The Kingdom Within
Light ✦ Light of the Eternal
Loving Your Problem ✦ The Narrow Way
The One ✦ Our Sufficient Guide
Our Victory ✦ Practical Demonstration
The Price of Glory ✦ Private Lessons
Science of Ascension ✦ The Seamless Robe
The Time Is at Hand ✦ The Understanding Series
The Voice of Revelation ✦ Who Am I
The Word Made Flesh

Available through:
Mystics of the World
Eliot, Maine
www.mysticsoftheworld.com

IN HIS NAME

A STUDY OF THE ABSOLUTE

Lillian DeWaters

I will give you a mouth and wisdom which all your adversaries shall not be able to gainsay nor resist.

—Jesus

In His Name

Mystics of the World First Edition 2014

ISBN-13:978-0692325094

ISBN-10: 0692325093

Published by Mystics of the World, Eliot, Maine

www.mysticsoftheworld.com

Cover graphics by Margra Muirhead

Printed by CreateSpace

Available from Mystics of the World and Amazon.com

DeWaters, Lillian, 1883 – 1964

Originally published:

Lillian DeWaters Publications

Stamford, Connecticut, 1926

Contents

PREFACE..7

CHAPTER I
   FACTS OF LIFE...11

CHAPTER II
   THE HIGHEST PRACTICE 49

CHAPTER III
   THE FAITH OF GOD 74

CHAPTER IV
   THE CHANGELESS CHRIST 105

CHAPTER V
   "NO CONDEMNATION" 137

CHAPTER VI
   REFLECTION..167

CHAPTER VII
   HEALING MINISTRY 199

ABOUT THE AUTHOR...205

When the disciple is ready the Master appears.

Preface

While the author was engaged in writing her book *The Christ Within* she was amazed one morning upon awakening to see suspended in the air above her head the words, "In His Name."

Clear, brilliant, dazzling they were. At first came the thought, "How wonderful they are! How warm and tender their message!" Then suddenly, "But what are they doing here? What do they signify like this?" Instantly came the answer: "The title for your next book!"

Thus it was that before I had completed the book upon which I was then working, ideas for the next book, whose title had been given me, were being revealed.

If one in New York wishes to be in Boston, there are various ways of traveling at his disposal. He may make the trip via trolley, or he might, if he wishes, journey by automobile or airplane. Now, man already lives in the Kingdom, yet, ignorant of this fact, he believes that he must take some means of arriving, and so we find various ways and methods open for his discrimination.

The Finished Kingdom is the way of pure metaphysics. *The Christ Within* is the way of devotion and self-surrender—the way of renunciation. *In His*

Name, while comprehending both these spiritual avenues, begins with the insight that man is all things here and now and that he is already in the Kingdom, needing no method of arriving.

In *The Finished Kingdom* the vision is toward the perfect Land, and this world of reality is called the finished Kingdom, not that in any way it associates with a period of time, but because its completeness is finished without a beginning and without an end.

The word *finished,* if viewed with a three-dimensional consciousness, will be connected with a beginning, and one might wonder how there could be an infinite God in a finished Kingdom, believing that since the Kingdom is finished, it must have been started or have had a beginning and therefore could not be infinite; but those of cosmic consciousness, those of larger vision, understand that the word *finished* is a fourth-dimensional term, beyond all sense of time, and means the finished or complete fact of being with neither beginning nor end—birthless, timeless, infinite, and eternal.

In *The Christ Within,* the vision is toward Self, the Jesus Christ reality, the perfect Being which man is. These two mentioned volumes present the Kingdom and the King, one and inseparable.

In telling of his trip in an airplane, one would use some particular phraseology, and were the journey made in an automobile, he would use, as it were, another language, a different set of words. In like manner, when one speaks metaphysics, he uses distinctive terms of speech, and when he expresses that which is beyond metaphysics, he must speak another tongue, a new language.

In this book, *In His Name*, the author brings the highest language that she knows. The highest practice is the science of Intelligence wherein that which *is,* is known to be *all* there is, and that which *is not* is known to be *nothing*.

As the science of the mentality, called the art of right thinking, is above and beyond the science of the body, called physiology, so the science of Intelligence is above and beyond the science of mind, or right thinking, and this book is written *in His name*—the name of Truth—that immortals may drink with me of' the river of the water of Life.

—The Author

Truth establishes you and holds you forever what you are. Rise, then, in your own name, which is His name, for there is none other name whereby you shall know emancipation.

In His Name, the name of Truth, behold yourself as you are, perceive Truth as Truth is. Then will you find yourself in the land of peace and wholeness and in the world of joy and delight.

— Lillian DeWaters

Chapter I

FACTS OF LIFE

True instruction comes with a message, comes with an announcement of that which *is*.

True instruction is based upon reality, is based upon the facts of Life. It comes not with methods and mental devices; it is neither in the wind nor in the whirlwind, but is the still, small voice of Truth.

It has been noted by the disciple that what he learns today he may discard tomorrow, and he wonders at the many shifts he seems to make and the many steps he seems to take in his progress heavenward.

Ascending a mountain at the top of which stands a great temple, one finds himself seeing and then discarding view after view. Commencing his journey, he may proclaim that the temple has one wing and one steeple; but, traveling longer, he discards this view and this conviction and states that the temple has three wings and five steeples.

Now, the temple ever remains the same, untouched by any view or belief about it, and though one declare five windows at one moment and fifty windows at another moment, he is not discouraged or ashamed because of this, but on the contrary he is rejoiced, knowing that as he ascends he is seeing more and more of the temple and that when he reaches the summit he will view the temple as it is.

It seems that in our journey heavenward, often we are ready and glad to discard one view for another and larger view of the temple of Life, and we should not be offended or ashamed because of this. Taking the upward view, we march on, forgetting the things that are behind and pressing forward to the full vision.

We boldly announce Truth when we know Truth, for it takes no courage to do this; it takes only the love and the joy of God. Walking in the supernal world, we can easily see and declare the facts of Life.

About fifty years ago, it was clearly and intelligently announced to the world that matter is nothing in and of itself. At the same time, it was presented that all is mind. Gradually this announcement gained attention until today there are millions of people who see the temple of Life this way: *There is no matter; all is mind.*

Now, to attain to this vision is a great step taken up the mountain; but to *stand* in this position, to see this view as the *extent* of our vision is disastrous.

To all those who reach this view that mind is all, to all those who see that what is termed matter is actually mind, or is mental—*and who see no farther than this*—there *must* arrive a moment when they will leap forward into a still higher and wider vision—the superb view that *all that is mental is nothing.*

To transpose the material world into a mental world is a step forward; but to have the insight that looks *in, under, above,* and *beyond*—that understands that because the material world is a mental world it is therefore nothing—this is the vision that rends the veil and announces:

> Truth is all there is, and that which seems to be and is not Truth, is nothing.

With spiritual vision time, space, distance, birth, duration, death, cause, creation, effect, sickness, sin, and change are all set aside, swallowed up, blotted out, remembered no longer in that great vision of the *allness* of Truth.

When the disciple is ready, the Truth is here, yet Truth requires open eyes and ready ears, that its message may be seen, accepted, and appreciated.

Many there are who, having heard affirmations and denials; having read various books presenting what is called Truth in various ways; having listened to sermons, lectures, and instruction month after month and year after year; having received instruction from teachers here and teachers there, become callous, hardened, unbelieving, unteachable, thus shutting the door to the light that is at hand, ready to burst through, for, "Except ye believe, ye cannot enter the kingdom."

Before one can have heat, he must have fire. If one has at hand the logs and the kindling, this is not enough, and he will still be cold, for he must also have the match, he must set the sticks afire, he must have the blaze. Then come the warmth and the glow and the heat. So, if one has the books, has the instruction, has the teacher, he will still feel himself in the cold, outside of heaven, unless he has *within himself the living flame,* the spark, the inspiration, the leap of joy, the bound of understanding.

The instruction, the teacher, the book act as the match that kindles in you the fire, that stirs in you the living breath, that quickens in you the ready spark, so that you know who you are and the Root from which you came. The fire is not in the book; the fire is in *you.* But the words, written or spoken, act as the torch to burn your heart, and with this burning you know yourself *a living Soul.*

Did not the words of Jesus act as this torch of light? For do we not read that as He spoke Truth to them their hearts burned within them? When written or spoken Truth fans the living flame within you and you feel the inrush of warmth, the flow of love, the melting down of barriers, the breaking away of bridges, the letting down of bars, then you know that you are receiving true instruction, that you are viewing the temple of Life in the right way.

As one understands the nothingness of mind, the nothingness of thought, the nothingness of mental creation, the nothingness of all except Truth, Reality, it is as though something had been removed; as though a covering had been taken off the eyes; as though one's whole being had been changed and the whole universe had been transmuted. Then one begins to walk in the light, to walk in the finished kingdom, to walk in the world of charm and magic.

To rest in the conviction that everything is mental has been thought and taught to be of very great advantage. To take all harm out of the thing itself and to place the harm in mind, as belief or appearance or idea, is considered by millions of people a very great step. To look at what is called disease and to say to a person, "This trouble is not in your body at all, but is wholly mental, that is, it is a false belief in your mind," is merely transposing the trouble from one position to another, is it not?

What advantage is it to consider pain mental rather than physical? No advantage, except that *by doing so you, perceive its nothingness.*

The three so-called planes of experience have been taken up and carefully explained in my work *The Finished Kingdom.* In continuance, we will say that those in the physical plane of living are conducting all experience upon the supposition that the external world and the things therein are reality, good and evil being in the thing itself, one thing having power over another thing.

Those who have discovered a superior position, the plane of mind, apply thoughts instead of things to the correction of all evils, to the solution of all problems.

For instance, if on the physical plane one thought or was told that a change of climate would be advantageous, he would move bodily from one state into another. In the superior position of the nothingness of matter and the allness of mind, one would not do this at all, but instead would make the change *in his mind*. He would now use *thoughts* of joy and gladness and happiness and health, for he believes that if he thus cultivates his mind, creating a change there from sickness to health, from despondency to delight, that his body will simultaneously undergo a corresponding change. This mental realm is clearly mind over matter, thought over body, and is the control of the body through and with the thoughts of the mentality.

Now, the translation of things into thoughts and the control of the body and its surroundings through the mind may enchant for a time; but the belief that disease is in the mind and that thought can control the body is not absolute Truth, and those entertaining this conviction are still ignorant or uninformed of the highest practice.

In the highest practice, the science of Intelligence, all that is mind is nothing; all that is appearance is nothing; all that is belief is nothing, and the mentality originating such ideas and such beliefs is also nothing.

If one can trace a condition to the mind, where it is called a false belief—*and leave it there*—that is, let the matter rest at this point or in this conviction that all falsity is belief in the mind, he has not yet seen all the Temple; he has further steps to take before the full Temple comes into view. He has not seen that which is *beyond the mind*, nor does he understand the highest practice of negation.

Let us leave the half-way position, the middle plane of mind over matter, thoughts over things, and let us with one bound leap to the high point and obtain the full view. Let us know that that which is Truth is unchangeable, untouched by any kind of thinking, either good or bad; that Truth is eternal, without beginning or end; that this Truth is *all there is*, and anything or any thought that does not measure up to this position of unchangeableness, eternity, *does not exist at all!*

In heaven, reality, the only world there is, there is no middle ground, and that which is, is all there is, and that which is not is nothing, does not exist at all. Mental denial is unnecessary; that is, one does not deny sin, sickness, appearance, belief in heaven, but he understands there is nothing to deny, for non-existence needs no denial. One must have the insight to understand that which does not exist is not present.

Multitudes are waiting to be shown the way to leave this middle ground of mind over matter for the highest position—the position which is beyond and above mind—*the position of Intelligence.*

Intelligence does not originate in the mind. Intelligence belongs to Soul, Self. The mind that can think both right and wrong, that can do both good and evil, that can see appearances called sin, sickness, and death—*this mind must be understood to be nothing.*

Mentality is simply another newer word for the human mind. Mentality, mind, mortal mind, human mind, carnal mind are synonymous terms, all meaning the human instrument or organ of thought. This mind is not Life or God and is not "divine Mind." Self is not mind, but Self is Mind, or Intelligence.

The human mentality must be perceived to be nothing in and of itself, and Intelligence, or divine Mind, must be understood as *all and only.* When it is said that we must know the nothingness of mind, it is meant that we must understand that the human mind or mentality is nothing in and of itself; it has no life or power or consciousness, and all that it originates is nothing, like unto itself.

The Mind that we are is the Mind of Intelligence and is the All-knowing or divine Mind, the Mind that was in Christ Jesus; and as we look over and beyond the human mentality with its creative thinking and comprehend Intelligence, or divine Mind, do we know and apprehend our true being.

When mentality is perceived to be nothing at all; when appearances are known to be nothing at all; when total negation is recognized and understood, then the so-called physical and mental condition can be instantly and absolutely erased.

When one has the insight to understand that that which is nothing is nothing; that a condition does not exist physically, does not exist mentally, does not exist in the body, does not exist as a false idea or supposition in the mind; when one can clearly perceive the nothingness of the flesh, the nothingness of the instrument called the mind, the nothingness of appearance, the nothingness of all that is not Truth, then he understands negation and has the power to erase permanently that which is called disease or difficulty.

This is the science of Intelligence, the science that is *above and beyond the mind*, the science that knows that which *is* and knows that which *is not*.

To transpose a material or physical condition into a mental or metaphysical condition and to heal with the conviction that the disease or difficulty is mental rather than physical or material is to bring about a transitory healing wherein one difficulty disappears for a time and then returns, either in the same form or in another name.

The science of Intelligence withdraws all attention from the body, withdraws all attention from the mind, withdraws all attention from the world of things and the world of thoughts, and the student discovers what he *is*, discovers his immortality, discovers his perfection, discovers his glory, his majesty, and his completeness.

To rush wildly here and there for our good, to strive vigorously with the mind for attainment of success and happiness is to be unenlightened and unmindful of the profound fact that *man is perfect now*, complete already, that Truth exists in being what it *is*.

When man learns the truth about himself, he does not see a great work ahead of him, a great attainment which he must achieve, great difficulties which are to be set aside through right thinking, but he understands that he is now a perfect being, without beginning and without end, that he is Intelligence, that he has the Christ-Consciousness now.

Man brings nothing from the outside to pour over him or pour into him, such as the memorizing and repeating of certain statements to be used as affirmations and denials which may result in creating what he desires, but he understands that his perfection is already established, that his perfection is unimpeachable, and that all he has to do is to know the reality of his nature and to expect and to enjoy a present perfect experience.

Instruction is not to make man over, not to change him in any way or to give him a more perfect and complete nature, but instruction is the river of the water of Life, and drinking therefrom, man finds his real nature to be Truth Itself and sees that it cannot be otherwise.

All limitations and false beliefs are mental. If you look into the distance and see the trees touching the sky, this is a mental illusion, *a mental creation.* So when you see deformity, illness, poverty and trouble, this is also mental creation, not the true reflection of Being, and man need not begin a housecleaning in his mind, sweeping out one idea with another idea so as to bring about a healing, for healing can take place without attempting to change the body and without attempting to change the mind. Healing takes place because man is already perfect and because mental creation is illusion.

This is the platform; this is the perfect practice; this is the science of Intelligence.

> This is the Science above and beyond the mind—to know that there is no body to be changed or altered and that there is no mind to be changed or altered, for man is immortal Being, above matter and above mind.

True instruction is the science of instantaneity, wherein one does not acquire health or success or harmony, either through matter or through any method of things or thoughts, but wherein one *is* all things and *is* all intelligence now and here. To perceive this is to have all that one desires, that is, to have immediately that which you wish, for you yourself are the fulfillment of all things.

Many are so tied to the mental method of thinking thoughts that they cannot comprehend the meaning of Jesus' words, "Take ye no thought," and, "Why reason ye?" for it seems to them that to let go their creative thinking and their reasoning would be the same as the giving up of their lives.

Truth cannot be defined. It is beyond and above all definitions, and no one by thinking can discover Truth or define Truth. As one has aptly asked, "Who by thinking can find out thought?"

Intelligence is not a state of the thinking instrument, but intelligence is a state of being, a state of reality. Intelligence does not think certain thoughts with the aim of attaining certain effects. Intelligence knows that nothing can be created either by right thought or by wrong thought. Intelligence knows that all that is, is *now* and nothing can be added to reality by right thinking, and nothing can be subtracted from reality by wrong thinking.

Reality remains the very same, no matter what one thinks or what one believes.

Thinking, so far as creating is concerned, accomplishes nothing, for how can one add to that which *All?* And how can one subtract from that which is changeless?

The perfect world is already eternally perfect in manifestation! That which is the reflection of Truth is like Truth, is without beginning and without end, and is unaffected by thought of any kind! The science of Intelligence has nothing to do with creation through right thinking or with malpractice through wrong thinking. All that is created through mind or by thought is an unreal creation, for anything that is created is begun, and anything that is begun is not Truth or reality, for Truth is *changeless.*

23

That all creation is mental, that all causation is in and of the mind, is correct, meaning that a mental creation is an unreal creation, is nothing, and a state of mind that is cause or that is caused is negation. To see this is to be lifted above mind into the realm of Reality; is to view the temple of Truth as it is, untouched by matter or by mind.

> The fact of Life is that we are immortals in heaven now.

Is not this a stupendous vision? A tremendous announcement? There is nothing to do. There is only something to *know*. "Ye shall know the truth, and the truth shall make you free." Ye shall know the truth, which is that you are already all that you ever will be, and to know this truth is to experience it.

> The truth that sets you free is the truth that you *are* free.

The moment you lose this vision or, ignorant of it, attempt to change your body through the avenue of your mind, that very instant you have ceased seeing the temple of Truth as it is and are attempting to "steady the ark," to add to or to take from that which is without any beginning and without end.

There is no progress to health. There is no change to reality. Completion is *now*. Fulfillment is *now*.

Now I have reached the height. *Now* I have reached the all that I wish. The word of Truth and full attainment is instantly transmitted.

Through the middle ground of mind over matter, through the stir and confusion of strife and conflict of thought, the man of insight walks undisturbed. He feels no movement or change. He knows that he is perfect and complete; he is all that he would be now. He knows that every man is Christ. He relies upon Spirit only; he practices healing through that which *is.* He sees no other; He sees only the One. He sees that each is all and all is each and that there is but One. *This is the All-in-all. This is the Lord of Hosts.*

No imperfection ever touches the body of man or the mind of man to make it other than what it is. As the fire pictured on the movie screen does not ever burn the screen, neither does that which is called blindness or deafness or disease or illness ever touch the perfect body. Nothing in the universe is ever harmed or injured, and one sees what is called healing brought to pass, demonstrated, not because man is sick, *but that the glory of God shall be manifested.*

Neither does this man sin, nor have his parents sinned, but ye shall perceive the nothingness of what is called sin and sickness and death, that ye shall know within yourself that perfection is on earth as it is in heaven.

Now, in heaven there is no healing taking place. Truth does not heal in heaven. Nothing is caused; there is no result. God cannot change; Perfection cannot change.

A woman came to see me for treatment. She had been under various forms of mental treatment for many years, without healing. She had read so much, she had heard so much, she had received instruction from so many teachers—she felt that she knew so much that she was callous, the same as if she had been encased in a hard shell. No matter what a teacher had said to her, she had previously known it. No matter what instruction had been delivered to her, she had already practiced it. Presenting herself to me, she asked, "You know that I can be healed, don't you?"

She expected me to reply, "Of course," which would have carried no weight whatever, for she had been so informed countless times. Therefore, I answered, "No, I know that you cannot be healed."

Now her face changed. A glimmer of attention came into her eyes. "Why, what do you mean that I cannot be healed? Certainly Truth heals!"

"No," I replied decidedly. "Truth never healed anyone. You will never be healed of this that you think is disease. You will never be other than you are this moment."

She straightened up and *listened*. Something in her began to stir, and she was moved. It seemed as though the hard shell were getting ready to crack open, as though the kindling were being prepared to make the fire.

"How can Truth heal a perfect being?" I continued. "How can I cause that to disappear which is not present? How shall I expect to awaken you who are already Intelligence and know all things? *How can that be done which cannot be done?*" Then illumination consumed the mist that was nothing; the fire flamed and burned within her, and she knew and experienced her completeness and perfection.

It is said by the illumined that the man of God accomplishes everything by doing nothing. One simply stands on the Rock that is Christ.

Truth sets one free from evil because there is no evil. *Believest thou this?*

All false manifestation is the result of false sense. False sense is nothing, and false manifestation is nothing. This is the cross. That which *is not* is so perceived, so understood, so known and accepted, thus is *crossed out.*

We are immortals living in heaven now. This is the world of heaven peopled with immortals—

but do they *believe* it? And except ye *believe* ye shall not enter into the kingdom of heaven.

Instruction is given with parables and illustrations that one may have the insight that looks beyond the veil. One of the illustrations which most clearly reveals the truth about immortals living in heaven is the illustration of the dream, which we will now consider.

One lies on a couch and enters that state called sleep. In this sleep he dreams that he is in the forest, making his way among the bushes and the trees. Suddenly he hears a peculiar sound, and peering ahead of him sees two brilliant spots like electric lights. Motionless he stands as these lights come creeping toward him, and soon a huge lion stands directly in his path. His heart begins pounding and racing: his legs are suddenly weak; he is so frightened that he cannot move his mouth to utter a sound. Slowly the animal comes creeping toward him, then leaping into the air, it is about to close upon him when he wakes to find, "It is only a dream."

Now, let us look deeply into this subject of the dream, for it carries a deep significance, deeper perhaps than you may at this instant imagine.

Who made the lion which the dreamer saw in the bushes? Who put that heavy mane on him and those blazing electric eyes and that wide-opened mouth? Only one—the man on the couch. He made the lion. He placed him in the bushes. He put the glare into those eyes and made him leap in the air to devour him.

Did he know that he was creating all this? Did he consider that the forest, the bushes, the fear that he felt, the weakness that came into his legs were of his own doing, his own creating? No, not at all. He thought it was all a creation outside himself and that he was in no way responsible for it and that he in no way could control it.

So while he is dreaming, he does not know that he is dreaming. This is one thing of which he is ignorant. And there is another thing that he does not know. He believes that he is in the dense forest, with his feet on the cold earth, and is unaware that he is in his own room with his body reposing on the warm couch.

Thus we see the two great facts of which he is ignorant. He believes that he is where he is not, that he is seeing and feeling and doing what he is not seeing and feeling and doing, and he is totally ignorant of the truth of that which is actually taking place—that he is in his own room safe and sound.

Let us see how this applies to the day dream, the dream of living in a material world, an external world outside our thought or control, a world of matter and mind. One finds himself, we will say, suffering with what is called rheumatism. He is unable to move about freely without pain. He does not know what created this rheumatism; he certainly has not the faintest suspicion that he is the creator of it.

While he is dreaming of the pain or the fear that is confronting him, he is ignorant of two things, the same two things as in the night dream. He is ignorant that sickness is a mental creation, a mental illusion, and he is ignorant of the fact that he is not a sick or fearful man, but that he is an immortal being in heaven.

As the man on the warm couch believes himself in the cold forest encountering a lion, so man, dwelling in the land of delight and harmony, thinks that he is a mortal on earth confronted with difficulties and troubles. As before stated, there is no change to take place; there is no adjustment to be made. There is only something to know, and this knowing consists in understanding total Reality to be all there is and in understanding the truth of total negation, the truth of that which is not.

Now, there are two ways in which one may rid himself of his dream at night, in which one may separate himself from his night dream. The most obvious way, of course, is to waken from his sleep, to come into knowledge of that which actually is. The other way is that he shall know while he is dreaming that he is dreaming. It is possible for one while dreaming to waken himself from sleep, consciously, and it is possible for one while dreaming to know that he is dreaming.

One time I dreamed that I was in a large open field, together with a party of children, plucking flowers. Looking up, I saw a cow approaching and was dreadfully frightened. I seized the hand of a child near me preparatory to running away, but just then I paused and said to the child, "Let us wait a moment. This may be only a dream. Now, if this is a dream, look, and you will see that cow vanish."

All the dream needs is that the dreamer suspect its unreality, and it is the same as though one walked away from the mirror—the likeness in the mirror also disappears; the dream is gone. I did not see the cow disappear, for the entire dream was instantly cut out, although I did not waken.

At another time I dreamed that I was in great trouble; that all those about me were in danger and peril. I myself was terrified, and none of us knew how to escape the impending disaster. Suddenly I stood in the midst and cried, "You people think this is all real, that there is no way out of this trouble. *There is a way out!*" Then I commanded myself, "Wake up! I tell you, wake up!" And immediately, there I was in the bed, straining my eyes open.

Since it is possible to consciously awaken oneself from a night dream and find the self safe in the room, so is it possible to awaken oneself from the day dream and understand that man is perfect in heaven.

At night one plays the part of entertaining the king or traveling in an airplane or swimming in the ocean and becomes so engrossed, so completely consumed with such ideas that he forgets who he is, that is, forgets his actual identity. He may be having a wonderful time with a party of young people, believing that he himself is young and free, forgetting entirely that he is a married man with a family.

Can it not be also, as one plays the part of a sick man or a poor man in the day dream, that he entirely forgets his real identity, that is, that he is an immortal being, perfect and harmonious, living in the real world of heaven?

It is possible for one to apply the same measures for waking from the day dream as one applies in his sleep to dispel the night dream. Suppose that one is daydreaming that he is sick and miserable; then let him pause, saying, "I suspect this is only a dream, an illusion. There is no reality in this thing at all, no more now than there is at night. I dream at night that I am traveling over the continent without ever moving from my bed; I see people with my eyes tightly closed; I hear sounds when my room is quiet and still. So in the day time, I feel pain when there is no pain present; I feel sorrow when there is no cause for it whatever. I realize that this is only a dream, an illusion, that it is wholly mental or is a state of mind the same as the night dream, and being a mental creation, it is nothing."

It is a fact that sickness and all difficulties are of the same nature in the day dream as in the night dream, and to see their total negation is to completely lose them, for all that preserves the dream of sickness and trouble is one's belief that it is something outside his own mind, that it is something rather than that it is *nothing*.

Yet as one in a dream at night does not comprehend that he alone is the creator of all that he is experiencing — that he makes the trees and the water and the cities that he sees, that he makes the people with whom he visits or talks, that he makes the streets upon which he walks, that he makes himself a victim, ignorantly — so one cannot understand that the sickness that he feels or the trouble that he experiences in his daily life is the same nature as a dream. Nor does he understand that such creation is no creation, that in its coming and in its going, nothing whatever is taking place.

> The dream and the dreamer are both nothing. Truth, Reality, Changelessness is all and must be so recognized and understood.

If one could learn how to make his dream as he pleases, as long as he is making it, what a great help this would be. For instance, I dreamed one night that I was in a room standing at a table upon which were placed some beautiful quilts. I picked up one, examining its texture and coloring, considering how delightful it would be for a certain room in my house. I did this with another and then with another, finding just the right places for the four quilts which were all there were on the table.

Looking up, I saw a woman standing near, watching me. She had such a longing in her eyes that I knew at once she wanted one of those quilts, that she actually needed one, while I only loved them for their beauty. I tried to make myself part with one of them, but seemingly could not, for I was selfish, and silently I watched her as, slowly and with manifest disappointment, she walked away.

At that moment I wakened, and taking in the whole situation, I said to myself, "You goose! You made those four quilts yourself; now why didn't you make another and give to that woman!" Do you see? As long as I made the four, why did I not make another for the woman, for I wanted her to have one. *I did not know that I made them.* I thought that someone else was responsible for them.

Is it not so in our daily experience? Do we pause to consider that as all creation is mental, it is easy enough to have what one wishes? And if we actually knew our being to be Truth, would we not know that all we had to do would be to make a wish and it would come true instantly? It would come true not because of the wish, not because of the thought or of the mind, but it would come true *because of the Self that we are,* for in the Self is all power and glory and dominion and majesty. Every wish is already fulfilled in the Self, Christ. Thus, it can "come true."

The fact of life is that man is what he *is.* He is not what he thinks he is; he is not what he believes he is; that is, neither his thinking nor his believing will make or unmake him. *Ever he will remain that which he is.* The much-quoted statement, "As a man thinketh, so is he," is not a fact of Life or Truth. In the world of delusion, in the world of mental creation, man is the sum total of his thoughts, or according to his thinking so does he manifest, but this is not true of Man, the Son of God.

As we lift our vision so that we view the temple of Truth from the heights, we clearly see that if thought made man, there would be an infinite variety of men instead of one man, Christ; and there would be beginning and change. When man thinks rightly, these thoughts do not establish his nature, do not make him other than what he was before he entertained such thoughts. Truth, true being, *your* true being is already established and is not affected by any thoughts that you may hold.

To be constantly on your guard to engage in a certain mapped out way of thinking is not freedom, but is slavery. If one must run to his mind for a thought when in danger or in trouble the same as one runs to his medicine cabinet looking over the labels "For headache" and "For colds," etc., he is in mental bondage. The notion that certain thoughts cause certain diseases and that to remove these diseases certain other thoughts must be employed as neutralizers, after the idea entertained on the material plane of swallowing one poison and then taking another poison as an antidote, has no place in the platform of Truth whatsoever.

All belief that there is such a thing as mental diagnosis in Truth must give place to the view of the full Temple, the insight and understanding that the power for good is not in thought and the power for evil is not in thought, that the only power there is, is Truth, which is undisturbed and unaffected by any ideas or by any mental creation whatsoever.

No one can add to Truth by certain thoughts, and no one can take from Truth by certain thoughts.

Students of understanding do not grope in the clutches of mentality; do not practice healing by the sending of prescribed cogitation; do not keep on hand an encyclopedia of catalogued diseases with certain scheduled thoughts for each particular case; but students of understanding practice healing, knowing that which *is* and that which *is not!*

No one can acquire Truth; no virtue is obtained this way. The way to come into possession of health, happiness, and any virtue is to know that it is *inherent in you,* that what you desire is *already* brought to pass.

Freedom, understanding, is eternal, inherent, not something to be acquired or attained. It is finished. And it is finished without a beginning and without an end.

> "*Now* I am a perfect being. *Now* I am free.
> *Now* all power and all changelessness are mine."

To utter thoughts like these as though the uttering or thinking of them thereby puts something into motion, brings something into view, causes something to be which is not at present on hand—to declare such thoughts with this idea in mind that they are power, that they are life, that they are causative is vastly different from announcing such thoughts *because they are true!*

The knowing of Truth is Truth and is not thought! Man knows because he is Intelligence!

Perception, insight, is not the controlling of the organ of thought, but perception looks over and beyond the mind, perceiving its nothingness and announcing that which is. Millions believe that mind is all. Mind, meaning *Intelligence,* that is, Mind with a capital *M,* is Truth and is *All,* but mind, meaning the instrument that seems to create evil, is nothing. Mental power is no power, for *all power is in Truth.* All power is Christ in you.

Can you see that the changing of your thought like the putting off of one garment and the donning of another has nothing to do with Reality? Whether you are wearing a velvet gown or are in rags, your being is the very same, is it not?

Can you see that the real man is above what he wears and above what he thinks? This does not mean that the man of Spirit is without thought, not at all; but it means that the Christ-Self, the man of God, does not consult his mind but looks above and beyond his mind, or the mental realm of change and birth and death, to Intelligence and to the perfect world of wholeness and completeness.

One cannot behold the universe of Spirit in which we live while he consults his body and his mind to find out how much of a man he is. Health and harmony are not a matter of becoming but are a matter of *being;* not a future state but a *present* state.

A mortal can never be transformed into an immortal by any choice selection of words or by any forceful ideas whatsoever. That which is, *is*, and that which is not, *is not*. Man has all now; man is all now that he will ever be, but does he believe it?

Because of this unbelief, a separation has seemed to appear, and those who do not believe in Truth—who do not believe in the perfection of being here and now, who do not understand the mental nature and unreality of sin, disease, and death and the fact that the kingdom of heaven is at hand—such as these are called "mortals," and it has been said of them that they must be born again.

This language, "Ye must be born again," is spiritual language, and the new birth is the consciousness that man is immortal; that he is like God, unborn; that within him is the living Christ. When this fire burns within him, he is said to be reborn, or born of the Spirit.

√   One has, in truth, a radiant body and a mind as clear as crystal reflecting that understanding which he is.

The putting on of the new man, the transformation of the mortal into an immortal is the *insight,* the perception that the children of God are the same as God.

As one in sleep can live the life of a king or can live the life of a beggar and thus be subject to his own mental creation, so on earth man lives the life of a mortal, being subject to the laws of matter and mind, and *new birth is his awakening to the perception of Truth,* is the burst of illumination wherein he sees and feels that Truth is all there is, and besides Truth there is nothing else!

√   The illumined consciousness does not speak of cause and effect, for it is known and understood that there is no such thing as cause and effect in heaven, the spiritual plane, the only world, for Truth is changeless and is all there is.

We have been told by great metaphysicians that all causation is mental. This is correct, but it should be added that causation, being mental, is thus unreal, illusion.

Since all causation is in mind like dreams, imaginations, pictures, beliefs, and these mental pictures are reflected and brought into manifestation like the images in the mirror—since such creation is in and from the mind, *such creation is not permanent and is not of Truth.* The seeming external world of illusion, the world of birth, sin, sickness, and death is therefore the creation of the subjective world of mentality and as such has both beginning and end.

Creation and effect imply beginning. Such infer a change, a starting, an impermanence. Now, since Truth is all there is and since Truth is changeless, there is no place in Truth for something to begin or be created, no place in Truth for cause and effect.

In the heavenly language, Truth is not a creator. The perfect world is the *reflection* of Truth rather than the creation of Truth.

All limitation is mental, that is, limitation is an imposition of the mind. There is no time, there is no space, there is no distance in Truth, which is *all there is.* All the changes that seem to take place from the cradle to the grave are brought about through *belief* and so are mental creation, transitory creation.

There is something in man that is untouched by material things and by mental beliefs; something in man that is never born, is never sick, never ignorant, and will never die; something in man over which the body and the mind have no control whatever; something which is apart from all

41

thinking, all acting, and all doing. This something is Intelligence, *is the Jesus Christ-Consciousness.*

In absolute language God, Truth, Jesus Christ, man are one totality of Being—one Life, one Intelligence, one Consciousness.

If one looks in mirrors of a certain construction, he may see himself very tall and very thin, or he may behold himself very large and very short, that is, he may view himself to be other than what he is. Now, one's mind is like a mirror, and when it is peaceful and quiet and calm, it reflects the Intelligence that one is. When it is disturbed and distorted and distracted, the picturization displayed is other than Intelligence, is other than the perfect, upright man of love, power, and majesty which one is. Such picturization is mental creation, mental illusion.

True instruction trains the mind to look upon things as they should be seen, to view life as it is, so that there will be no distortions; so that man's mind will image forth the truth about himself, that as he looks he will see himself as he is.

On the motion picture screen when we see a person running from one side of the picture to the other, our intelligence informs us that there is no such person there. When we see a man die, it tells us that nothing whatever has taken place. With intelligence we look at things which are not seen as though they were present, and we look at things which are apparently seen as though they were nothing.

The perfect world is not a mental creation but is the reflection of Truth, is present now, and what we need to do is to know this and to understand that mental creation is a superimposition which ✓ vanishes before understanding, as darkness is swallowed up by the light.

To distinguish between that which *is* and that which *is not* is insight, illumination. As soon as one actually knows the nothingness of nothing, the mist is gone; the yoke falls away, for *one cannot be held in bondage to that which he knows is nothing.*

The science of Intelligence delivers the message, announces that which is, and invites, "Come unto Me, ye who are shackled and heavily burdened. Come away from the world of matter and mind and enter the heavenly land, the realm of magical glory." *Believest thou this?*

> This insight that discerns that which is and that which is not is the fire which burns and consumes the chaff, which looks at appearance of sickness and deformity and declares, *"It is not there!"*

When you look into the mirror and see yourself very tall and very thin, you say to yourself, "This is not so," and you walk away, not deceived by such a picture. When you see one man injure another man on the movie screen, you say to yourself, "There is no truth in this whatever; nothing is taking place." You are not deceived by such a visual illusion. Then why are you deceived when you look at your body and see it other than you know it ought to be? You know that it ought to manifest perfection and harmony, and you should not be at all deceived if it appears that it is manifesting discord, but should know that nothing whatever has happened and hold to this true conviction of consciousness.

This conviction of the truth of that which is and the truth of that which is not came to me very clearly when first I took up the study of Science many years ago. I looked at what seemed a hopelessly sick animal at the point of death, and that animal immediately arose to its feet strong and well.

It happened one day while in the house, I heard the screams of children, the barking of dogs, and great commotion in the street. When I looked from the window, this was the sight which presented itself to my eyes: a cow was being dragged across the street on a stone-boat. The horses used for this purpose were frightened, the children were excited, and dogs were racing and running in great distraction. There was one man holding the cow's head to keep it from the ground, another man holding its tail, while others were busy keeping back the excited dogs.

I recalled that this cow had lain for several days in a lot near our house, having wandered away from its home. Veterinarians had been employed, and it had been decided that the cow was suffering with paralysis and would never be able to stand again, so now they were taking her to the stable to put her out of her misery in the most humane way.

As I looked from my window at this moving drama of discord and confusion, *this mental creation*, that moment came to me when I sat in the heavens and laughed. To think of that being a cow! Why, it was too absurd for words! There was nothing like that present at all! Nothing there at all but the perfect cow and the perfect order of heaven. *I felt it and knew it.*

I came away from the window, the incident entirely wiped from my mind. Later I was informed that when they reached the stables and were deciding how best to dispose of the cow, she suddenly sprang up on her feet and walked to her right place in the barn apparently strong and well. The next day she was grazing out in the pasture as though nothing whatever had taken place.

If you can have this vision that sees that which is and that which is not and have it like a blazing light, like a burning fire, so that you perceive and understand the total negation of false appearance before your eyes and see instead what you wish to see—wholeness, perfection, harmony—the action of heaven is transmitted, the dream is dispersed, the true vision is brought into view.

If you can look at what is called disease and discord and say intelligently and understandingly, *"It is not so! There is no such thing as evil in the universe"*—if you can *know* this, so shall it be done unto you.

There is no material action; there is no mental action; there is no action in the world of mental unreality or illusion. The only action there is, is the heavenly world, and this action is beyond the power of mind to describe.

When one is able to see the real instead of the unreal, the miracle always takes place. When one is able to lay aside all desire to correct the error by certain things or by certain thoughts; when one is able to see that when it is present it is nothing and when it is removed nothing whatever has taken place; when one can clearly and intelligently understand total negation, then the miracle is at hand.

A well-known English metaphysician taught this very clearly and in his noted book wrote the following:

> When anything is going wrong in the material world and you turn in thought and realize with sufficient clearness what is happening in the spiritual world, this recognition of the action of God results in what is called a miracle—the material trouble is put right. ... If anyone will lose all sense of the material world, realizing with sufficient clearness the omnipotence of His perfect action in the perfect world, heaven, he will be healed *instantaneously* (Frederick Rawson).

The following quotations are from the textbook of another great teacher:

"It breaks the dream of disease to understand that sickness is formed by the human mind, not by matter or by the divine Mind" (Mary Baker Eddy). This means that sickness is a false creation of a false mind and as such has no part in Intelligence or Reality.

"Revelation will destroy the dream of existence ... ushering in the glorious fact that both man and woman proceed from God and are His eternal children. ..." (Mary Baker Eddy). That is, *insight* will look through the dream existence, perceiving its nothingness, and will view reality, the temple of Life, as it is. The miracle then takes place—man finds himself like God.

"Entirely separate from the dream of material existence is the Life divine" (Mary Baker Eddy). The realm of the material and the realm of the mental have no reality, no actuality. The only realm there is, is the divine.

"Sickness is a dream from which the patient needs to be awakened ... Mortal existence is a dream ... The dreamer and the dream are one, for neither is true nor real ... That which is termed disease does not exist" (Mary Baker Eddy).

Sickness is a dream, and a dream is nothing, has no actuality. That which is called disease exists only in mental creation or in the dream world and is therefore the same as any dream—is nothing.

In the chapters following we will proceed to present the application of the facts of life to daily experience. We now briefly summarize the platform of Being:

> God and man are one. Man is unborn, immortal, dwelling in the perfect world. There is no cause and no effect in matter, in mind, or in Truth; hence, cause and effect are nothing.
>
> The perfect world is the perfect reflection of Intelligence. Matter and mind, being nothing, having no power, cannot set disease aside, but Intelligence sets it aside by knowing and understanding its nothingness, to the glory of God.
>
> That which is, is Truth, and is all there is. That which is not Truth is negation.

Chapter II

THE HIGHEST PRACTICE

Truth is good. Truth is unchangeable, indivisible, and It is all there is. All miracles are based on the perception that God, Truth, is all there is, that is, all miracles are based on the allness of goodness and perfection.

Demonstration is a word which implies that there is something to do, a sickness over which one is to demonstrate, something which is to be eradicated or changed. First of all, let it be understood that what is called a miracle or a demonstration does not take place in the perfect world of Truth. Truth is already established, and this fact must so fire the consciousness that one will not speak of a method of healing or a process to be executed or any change to be effected.

To set to work as though you expected to accomplish something by a method of thinking; as though you anticipated bringing about a certain effect or result by meditation; as though there were a problem set before you to solve or a work set before you to do—this is to turn your back to the Temple, to forget who you are. It is to shackle yourself before you begin. Anything, any method, any thought that you use with the idea of making Truth true, bringing Truth into manifestation, is a hindrance to you, is a yoke upon your neck, for *Truth is that which is so already.*

Many write asking, "What thought shall I hold for this trouble?" Or, "What is the best treatment for this disease?" It would seem as though such could not lift their vision high enough to understand that the instant one attempts to use his thought the same as he would administer a particular powder for a certain disease, that instant he has turned from Truth.

To consider what you shall think to deliver yourself; to consider how you shall change your mind to bring out harmony; to consider the best mental method to use to cause a swelling to reduce, a boil to discharge, or a fever to break into perspiration—this is to blindfold yourself before you start. It is as though you were getting ready to run a race, and before you start you place a heavy load upon your back and shackles upon your feet.

The moment you consider, "What process of thought or reason shall I employ?" that moment you are looking down instead of looking up, and there is no wonder that such blindness holds you to your dream. Demonstration does not take place because of any words, because of any ideas, because of any meditation, because of any concentration.

Demonstration takes place because of Truth, because of the fire in you, because of that which you are.

If, as you are sitting in a train which is standing still, you watch another train moving past, you will commence to feel that you yourself are moving. You will feel that it is your train that has started and is slowly moving forward. The way to prove this is to turn your gaze from the train at your side and let it rest on your other side, on the standing objects, such as the trees and the buildings which you know are still. You will then find that you are not moving at all, that the motion you feel and see is a mental illusion, a mental creation, a superimposition.

Now, as in the train you turned your attention from that which is in motion to that which is still, so you must do when in seeming trouble of any kind. Turn your attention from that which seems to be moving and look at that which is *fixed*, which is *changeless*, which is *Truth*.

If, for instance, you see what is called a fever, the moving of the blood into the face and surface of the body, you do not question, "How shall I correct this fever?" You do not wonder, "How shall I manage the mind so that this fever is reduced and a perspiration begins?" But looking away from all this motion, illusion, and turning

51

your face to the Light, you say: "There is no fever in Truth. There is no change in Truth. There is no cause, no effect, nothing transpiring, nothing happening. There is only *isness*, purity, goodness, wholeness, unchangeableness, health, strength, insight, power, and glory; and this is *all* there is, and this is omnipresent at all times and so is here now, and there is nothing else here. Everything is just as it ought to be!"

Where is Truth to be found if not in yourself? In the Life that you are? In the Intelligence that you are? Look to this Life and this Intelligence within you and announce what is true and make your treatment seem as an announcement, an acknowledgement, rather than as a dose of mental medicine which you are administering to cure a mental disease or disorder.

We have heard that as Truth is all there is, that right in the spot where the pain or the trouble seems to be, Truth is there, for Truth is omnipresent. How can this be? Is the pain the Truth? Is the swelling the Truth? Shall we say since Truth fills all space, then this swelling is Truth? For what else could it be, if Truth is all? What else could the swelling be, if not Truth? Is this our announcement?

Ah, no! No such announcement comes from the perfect vision, our Intelligence. We do not thus apply Truth to our phenomenal experience. This would be the same as declaring that darkness is light, that ignorance is intelligence, and that discord is harmony. The announcement is this:

> Right in the place where the pain or difficulty seems to be, Truth is, because the condition is nothing! Truth is all!

Light is all; darkness is nothing. Intelligence is all; ignorance is nothing. Harmony is all; discord is nothing. Truth is cancellation of anything that is not like unto Itself. *Truth is all there is, and there is nothing besides.* There cannot be Truth and fever, and then in some way Truth has power over fever. The Truth is the only presence; the fever is no thing, nothing, negation.

In this vision you do not question, "Is not this disease too hard to heal? Will not this disorder take a long time to remove?" You now understand how all disease and disorder are alike, all nothing, and that you are perfect now and here; that no matter what seems to be where Truth is, it is not there, for *Truth* is *all* there is. "*I* am Truth, and besides Me there is none else."

You are to know, when someone presents himself to you for treatment, that a perfectly well man has come and that he will walk out of your office not changed in any way. He cannot change, for he is *changeless*. You do not see a sick man and administer treatment to him; you do not think of him as your "patient." *You see only immortals in heaven, and you know that a dream is nothing.* You do not treat a person or a mentality or a body. You merely announce Truth to Truth! Life is the I AM. Intelligence is the I AM. This cannot change, cannot be other than what it is, and *this is totality.*

The science of instantaneousness means that the healing has *already* been done. "It is finished. ... There is now no condemnation to those who are in Christ Jesus. ... Ye shall drink any deadly thing and it shall not hurt you. ... Be ye therefore perfect, even as your Father which is in heaven."

To lose the notion that there is something to heal brings one power and strength. There is no coming of something that one does not already have. You cannot be more perfect than you are now. *Believest thou this?*

Thus it is said, "Before they call, I will answer." Before you give or receive a treatment, you are already healed. There is nothing to change; there is only something to *know.* There is no separation; there is no distinction between God and man. There is but one Truth, one Life, one Intelligence, one Self, one I AM, one Presence, and I am this. I do not speak with mind. I do not create thoughts. I speak Truth. I speak the Word. I am the fulfillment of that which I AM.

Now, as there are three so-called sciences, though but one is actual, we will consider the treatments used in each.

The material science directs the treatment to what is called the sick object—the *body*—and the treatment of the body is called the *objective method*.

Next we come into the mental field, in which tens of thousands find themselves today. Here it is the *mind* that is treated. It is taught that the trouble is not in the body at all, but the trouble is in the mind as wrong belief. Reaching the body through the mind is mind over matter and is the *subjective method*, that is, the changing of the mind is termed the subjective way or mental method.

Lastly we come to the highest science, that of the Absolute, wherein there is no objective method and no subjective method employed; wherein there is no change to take place in the body, and there is no change to take place in the mind; wherein neither is objective body nor subjective mind considered cause or effect.

In the science of the Absolute it is intelligently known and understood that there is no actual healing to take place; there is no actual achievement. Consciousness is lifted above and beyond both mind and body to Soul, Self, Truth, and one is to "know the Truth," know the truth of Being, the truth of Life, the truth of Intelligence. One is to have insight to see that which is *as it is* and to know its totality and discern the total negation of all else that purports to be—and is not— Truth.

When one comes to you for help, do you begin in your mind like this: "Now, let me see, what are the best thoughts to think about this condition or this state of mind so as to quickly help this individual out of his difficulty"? Do you now discern that in having such a vision as this you are already considering a sick being? That you have pronounced sentence upon him before you begin a treatment?

Do you attempt something like this when one presents himself for treatment: Do you turn over the pages of some book of metaphysical diagnosis, letting your glance run along until you reach the name of the disease or trouble which one claims to be manifesting, and, reaching this name, do you read the best thoughts to hold to heal this condition or to change this state of mind? Do you outline right ideas for another to hold that will bring about a change in the mind, expecting this change in the mind to reflect a corresponding change in the body?

This is not viewing the full temple of Truth and is not the highest practice. Yet we condemn no way, for there is nothing to condemn. We point out Truth so that others ready and waiting for the highest practice may see and understand—so that immortals may drink of the living Fountain.

The highest practice of the hour is to know that there is no such thing as sickness, injury, disaster, or trouble, and that *there is no one believing in such things*. Right treatment is the acknowledgment of the facts of Life; the unity of Being; the announcement of that which *is*.

The body cannot answer the question, "Who am I?" The mind cannot answer, "Who am I?" Only Soul can answer, "I AM THAT I AM, and besides Me there is none else." I am not the body. I am not the mind. I am Self, Intelligence. This is my real being. The *I* that I am is *all* that I am. Nothing can be added to flesh to make it Spirit. Nothing can be added to mind to make it Intelligence. Nothing can be added to Self to make It greater than It already is.

In the subjective method of treatment, one is allowed to tell his practitioner his thoughts regarding his body and his state of mind. He then uses the words *false appearance* instead of the word *disease*, and it is understood by him that the cause for this false appearance is in his mentality.

Looking higher than this, we do not see discord and call it "appearance" or "supposition," for does changing a name bring us any nearer Truth or nearer Reality? In saying "belief of headache," does this terminology bring relief more quickly than to say "headache"?

Of what advantage is this transposition of terms or the translation of things into thoughts? If things are thoughts and thoughts are things, as we have been taught, then in what way do they differ? And what advantage is it to say you "thought" you were sick rather than to say that you were sick?

The point is this: the transposition of terms will never satisfy. There is bound to arrive a moment in your life, if you are earnestly seeking Truth, when this translation of a material world into a mental world will not be sufficient for you; when you will feel that there must be something higher; when trouble will continue and will force you to accept a higher vision, that you shall know Truth as Truth is.

If things and thoughts are the same, then what difference does it make whether you call disease a thing or a thought? And what difference whether you use the objective method of healing things with other supposedly more powerful things, or healing thoughts with other supposedly greater thoughts? In both instances one holds the idea that there is something to be healed, something to be set right. In the objective method it is the body, while in the subjective method it is the mind.

Now, do you think disease minds whether you call it "rheumatism" or "belief in rheumatism"? Do you think it cares whether you place pain in the foot or in the mind? As long as you name it, as long as you place it, is not this all it asks? And so long as you give it a name and make a room for it, will it stay with you where you have placed it. Does it seem strange to you now that you have never seen it like this before?

When you are in great suffering, do you think it makes it easier for you to understand that the pain is in your mind only? Do you think that Truth can make the pain go out of your mind more easily than out of your body? Do you think that to know that "all is mental" is all that Truth requires of us? That this view of Truth is the highest vision? That this will cause error to depart? Indeed, the translation of the material world into a mental world is not all that is required of us; it is not the highest practice; it is not the way of Intelligence.

We must look over the mind as well as look beyond the body. We must see Truth as It is and see all such erring suppositions and such mental ideas as nothing—in fact, less than nothing. We do not say then, "There is only a false appearance here," but with the vision of Truth in our hearts we announce:

"There is no such thing as false appearance! There is no such thing as erroneous supposition! There is no false mind here. There is no mind to conceive falsity! There is no false body here. There is no appearance here. There is no supposition here.

There is only Truth here, and Truth is all there is. Truth is perfect and all action is perfect. The body is perfect. Mind is perfect. Soul is perfect. There is no appearance to change. There are no false ideas to correct. There is nothing but God, Truth, which is all there is!"

Oh, marvelous vision! Oh, glorious understanding! No wonder the illumined say that he does the most who does nothing. Knowing is not doing. Knowing is *being*. Knowing is the piercing light, the burning flame, and what is healing but a flash of light—the light wherein we see and know as we are seen and known?

One time I was called to give treatment to one who had tried many healing methods, but the light had not dawned, the healing had not taken place. At this time, I, too, looked at the trouble, calling it "appearance only," believing that "it is all mental, false belief only"; but the demonstration was not made. Then one day it came to me like this: "I must know more than this; this is not enough. God, send me more light; send me all the light I need, that I understand all that is required of me to meet this case." This was what I asked.

Within a few hours I understood that which I should know. The Light came to me through something which I read, something which just at that time was sent to me. In that hour, as I read, I saw clearly and intelligently that all that is mental is nothing; that by renaming disease, nothing is accomplished. I saw that thought in itself is nothing, that right thinking can accomplish nothing that is not *already* done, and that wrong thinking is utterly without power, is negation.

I saw that all that is needed to put a face in the mirror is for one to place himself before the mirror; that all that is needed to cause the face to vanish from the mirror is for one to walk away; that is, all that is needed to place disease in the body is for one to make a place for it and call it by some name, to tabulate it in some way.

I saw that no matter what seemed to be in the body as disease, it is nothing, the same as the face in the mirror is nothing. I saw the world of illusion to be like the pictures on the movie screen — nothing. I saw the perfect universe to be the reflection of Truth. I saw that all that is needed to cause the trouble to vanish from the body, as the face does from the mirror, is *to have the insight to behold the nothingness of that which is nothing!*

I saw all this and more; and in that hour when I knew that all is Intelligence and besides Truth there is nothing else, in that hour I was the burning fire, the devouring flame, the flash of light, the illumined Soul; and in that same moment word came to me that the one who had asked for help was instantaneously and completely healed.

Now, the instant you look into Reality, seeing It as It is, knowing Self as also you are known, beholding the Christ-Consciousness as totality, that moment the action of the spiritual world is felt. It is the same as while looking at one picture on the movie screen, a picture of anguish and trouble and terror, immediately there flashes from out that picture another scene, a scene of laughter and joy and radiance. When one knows the nothingness of nothing, then what is called disease vanishes, for all that has given it a seeming has been taken away.

Today a well-known teacher of the Absolute clearly voices the way of Truth in the following: "Instruction in Truth is a message and not a method. It is not a procedure either subjective or objective. It is the hearing of the Truth. It is not thought that cures us of error. It is the knowledge of Truth which is Truth Itself. That is different from mind changing. Perception is the renunciation of the mind. Thought does not create anything, much less Truth. Nothing is created, Truth being all. For what reason were you informed that all is mind?

That you should understand that mind is Truth? No. So that when the message of Truth came to you stating that birth, sin, sickness, trouble, bondage, and all vicissitudes up to death are all mental creations, that in the perception of the nothingness of mind you would be able to see the nothingness of your troubles. There is no such thing as a mental substance. Substance is Truth. Consciousness of Truth is the only substance there is, and mental creations are nothing."

It can be easily accepted that there is no matter, all is mind. That is, what is termed material, like a house and a rug, is mental. But matter, being reduced to mind, should not be left in this state. Are we to hold that a house is not real as matter but is real as mind? Are we to hold that disease is not real as matter but is real as mentality? Now, if we believe that all is mind, then mind becomes reality to us. Is this not so? And if mind is real and disease is mind, then disease would be as real as mind, would it not?

Unless one takes the step upward and perceives the *nothingness* of all that is mental, he is not viewing the temple of Truth as it is. Let us look very closely at this, for it is a marvelous step forward, unknown today by millions in the mental field of procedure.

It is not difficult to see that every manifested thing from a pin to a palace first existed in the thought before coming into form, that is, all things existed as thoughts at one time; all things were in the mind as ideas before taking external form. As what is called a thing was first a thought or an idea, so all things are thought forms or thoughts manifested or externalized.

The word *material* means "not of mind," and since there is no inanimate thing in this whole universe that is not born of mind, since mind conceived all external inanimate things in the universe, then it is easy to see that "nothing is material, for all is mental." We seemingly live in a mental world, all experience being mental and nothing else.

What is a thought? What is an idea in the mind? Is it anything at all?

If I have in my mind an idea of a lion, can this lion run out into the street and stop the traffic? If I think in my mind that I will go downtown, will I by thinking this be able to go into the stores and bring home some groceries and merchandise? If I conceive in my mind that the town hall is burning, will this idea ring in the firm alarm?

Can you see that a belief is nothing? That a thought is nothing? That an idea is nothing?

Since disease is then understood to be belief in the mind only, idea only, thought only, then why can one not take the next step and see that *because disease is belief and thought only, it is therefore nothing, for that which exists in the mind as belief is nothing at all—nothing at all.*

That which is true, which is changeless, which is unborn and undying does not exist in the mind, but *is,* and is *in spite of the mind.* Can you accept this great fact—that disease and discord, being in and of the mind, are nothing, absolutely nothing? That anything which springs from the mind as belief, opinion, thought, idea is nothing whatever? Truth does not originate in the mentality. Truth is above the mental instrument, and only that which is Truth is actuality and power.

The mentality does not originate Truth, but *reflects* Truth. The knowing of the Truth is Intelligence, not mind, and Intelligence is changeless. The mind that believes in good and evil, right and wrong, that can think sickness and sin—this mind belongs to the world of unreality, the dream world, and does not belong to that which is Truth. All that is good and true springs from Intelligence, divine Mind.

Now, to understand that all that is matter is really mental and all that is in and of the mind is nothing—this is the highest practice; this is the art

65

of negation. To actually grasp this truth of negation is to be instantly freed from disease or discord that one seems to experience. To understand that there is no power in an idea, no power in belief, does not mean that one must not continue to have right thoughts and right ideas, not at all; but it means that you shall place things where they belong, that you shall place things in their right position. It means that you shall express ideas and thoughts, yet know all the time that all the power there is, *is in Truth*. As the electric power is in the power house and not in the electric wire, so all the power there is, is in Self, I AM, and is in nothing else.

To briefly review, we find, then, that all is Truth and Truth is all, and all that seems to be and is not Truth is nothing; that appearance is nothing, change is nothing, belief is nothing, matter is nothing, mentality is nothing, flesh is nothing—in short, anything that is subject to change is not Truth, for Truth is *changeless*. All that is perfect without beginning or end, all that is complete and finished without birth or death, all that is indivisible, all that is reality and purity, is Truth.

He who lives in this insight lives in the light. He who lives in the mentality lives in darkness, in prison, and is bound and tied by his own thought creations, a slave to them, knowing not freedom and liberation. He uses the same instrument, mind, to kill and to cure. Emancipation is never obtained through the mind. A great many people have found themselves worse off after they left matter for mind. Why is this? Because it is easier to get away from a thing than it is to get away from a thought.

For instance, if you do not like the house in which you live, it is easy enough for you to move into a more desirable home; but supposing that you do not like the thought of fear that you have in your mind—how can you escape it? Can you run away from it? Will moving into another location take the fear from your mind?

Can you conceive of anything more heart-rending than for a mother to believe that her own fear is causing the sickness of her child, yet be unable to master this fear? And are we not taught that fear is the cause of sickness? For a mother to believe that her fear is the cause of the child's suffering is for her to be in bondage, darkness.

Is there anything more pitiful than to see one bound hand and foot to thoughts from which he longs to escape, yet believing all the time that his thought is creative and is power? How can you, with thought, release yourself from thought? One who is thus blinded is his own victim.

It is time that one clearly understands that *fear is nothing!* That fear is not creative! That fear can do nothing whatever, for it is nothing at all! Fear-thoughts of others cannot harm you, nor can your fear-thoughts harm others. If you *know* this, you are knowing Truth, and to believe other than this is to tie yourself, shackle yourself to something from which you must later escape.

Does not this enlightenment take a great load from your shoulders? Do you not feel a great weight being lifted from your mind and a great joy flooding your being, to be told and to intelligently comprehend that there is no power whatever in the mentality? When you see that all power is in Truth and is in nothing else, then you learn what emancipation is. What greater hell can one experience than to believe that his own thoughts are creative, injuring himself and others whom he loves, and yet be powerless to control them?

You will notice that when great fear is depicted on the moving picture screen, that such fear is nothing; that the man who is running to escape the danger is doing nothing, for there is no danger there, and in fact, there is no man there. If you attempt to touch this curtain with your hand, you will touch only the white sheet. It is like this in the night dream. The things you see exist only in the mind, and being in the mind, are nothing at all. *All that is a picture, a shadow, a reflection is not anything at all.*

This world that seems about us, this world of change, of birth and death, is but a cinema, a dream world with no more reality than the world that is depicted on the movie screen. The world of reality is the world of perfection, of charm and beauty, of love and glory, of peace and plenty, of changelessness and eternal joy. When we fix our vision upon this perfect world, it seems as though it springs right out into view, right into and out of this mental world that is seen about us, so that the birds are more wonderful to us, the flowers are more beautiful, and all living things take on a grander glow; the same as while one is looking at a picture on the screen and another seems to come right out of it or into it, another of contrasting glory and charm.

True manifestation is not created. Mental creation proceeds from mind instead of Spirit. Truth being all there is, creation then is only in the world of appearance, the world of imagination, and as such is impermanent, unreal. The perfect world which is the reflection of Truth is not a creation, but like Truth is unborn, unending.

It is in the world of creation, the cinema world, that disease has appearance, healing, and disappearance; that people are born and die. None of these changes take place in the true world, or heaven, and their happenings are like any dream, for there

69

can be nothing but changeless Reality. Now, it is this perception that is needed—this perception of the allness and the oneness of Truth, the allness and totality of Self, of Life, of Intelligence, and the nothingness of all else.

One does not have to pound his fists on the arms of the chair or use vigorous terms of speech to know Truth; such is not the message of Truth, wherein Truth sets you free from evil because there is no evil! You do not hammer evil thoughts; you do not pounce upon erroneous suppositions, but you lift your vision high enough to behold their nothingness.

Though I heal ten thousand cases of diseases and cause them to disappear from the body, and though countless times I change the mind from one idea to another, if I am unaware that I have thereby accomplished nothing, I know not Truth. Though I transform thoughts into things and things into thoughts ten thousand times and know not that in doing this nothing has taken place in reality, I know not Truth. When my mind is placid like a crystal lake, my mind fulfills itself, reflects like a mirror the Intelligence which I am.

If I strive to be master, I shall never attain; if I aim to be, I shall never arrive; if I look up and away to a power outside and beyond Myself, I shall never find. Only when I know as I am known shall

I find that *I*, Self, the *Jesus Christ character*, am Master. *I*, the one Life, the one Intelligence, am Spirit, Truth. *I*, the one and the all, the unborn and the undying, am the power and the glory, the living Reality.

It is not, "I will be master," but it is, "I *am* master." It is not, "I will succeed," but it is, I *am* success. It is not, "I will have health," but it is, "I *am* health, wholeness, perfection. I am all life, all intelligence, all good, all glory, for the only *I* there is, is I AM THAT I AM. God, Father, Son, Christ, Jesus, Life, *I*, Intelligence, Soul, Spirit, Love, Being, One, Totality are synonymous terms, all meaning the one God, the one I AM, for besides this, there is none else.

If I am one with the highest, I am the highest, for God and man cannot be separated. The Kingdom is within. The King is within. The living Christ is within. There is no time, no birth, no death for this King or for this Kingdom. My eye beholds this King of glory, with face as the sun and with raiment as the light, filling all being with His presence, filling all that is called space with His power, and radiating, reflecting peace, beauty, joy, abundance.

Now, the mind is not to seize this truth, but this truth is to seize the mind. The mind cannot behold the spiritual world in which we now live except the mind have a vision, except the mind be pure and clear, except it renounce itself—taketh no thought, but simply reflect the facts of being.

Whenever pain leaves the mind, no void is left; nothing has been taken away. Nothing has taken place when the flowers leave the mirror. The mirror remains the same when the flowers are there as when they are gone. Thus, the coming and the going of ideas in the mind signify nothing at all as taking place. They occupy no room; they are nothing.

Does not the coming of this Truth to your consciousness bring angels, miracles, signs of Its presence? Does not your whole being cry out in agreement that Truth is, "Yea, yea" and "Nay, nay"?

Rebirth is this illumination, this discovery that you are a perfect being, an immortal now in heaven. With this illumined consciousness you fall not under the lash of the law, but you have the insight that looks above and beyond the dream world, the world of methods and processes, and sees clearly and intelligently that nothing can be added to or subtracted from the Truth which you are.

There is nothing that shall harm you in all My holy mountain of Reality, for the earth is filled with the knowledge of Truth, and no man shall ask, "Show us the Truth," but each shall know in his own heart, "I am the Truth, I am the Light, and besides Truth there is none else."

"There is therefore now no condemnation to those who are in Christ Jesus," those who know that Christ Jesus and God the Father are one and the same; that a trinity is a unity; that Father, Son, and Holy Ghost—Spirit, Man, and heaven—are identical.

Of what value are words to you, no matter how marvelous they sound, except you apprehend their meaning? Except you appropriate them? What value is the richest food to you except you partake of it? And except ye eat of My flesh, (perceive this Truth)—I AM—ye have not yet known Truth as Truth is, for the eating of My flesh is the perception of the living Word, the discernment of perfect, complete, immortal being now and here.

The Word is not spoken that something may thereby take place. The Word is spoken to behold the Light that is shining; to behold the Fire that is glowing; to behold the Christ-Self—*the Highest and the Inmost the same.*

Chapter III

THE FAITH OF GOD

Since there is but one Life, one Intelligence, one Consciousness, one Christ, then what is birth? What is death? What is resurrection?

Can Spirit be born? Can Intelligence be created? Can Life die and be resurrected?

Will you open your vision, stretch your mind to behold Truth, Self, to be *uncreated, unborn?* Will you acknowledge this truth, this fact of being: *I,* Soul, Spirit am unborn, uncreated; *I,* Truth, Self will never die and will never be resurrected. Will you leap to this vision? Will you proclaim, "Yea, yea, it is so?"

Are you a character in the book? Are you a picture in the mirror or a shadow on the walk? If so, then you are nothing, for the character in the book, the reflection in the mirror, the shadow on the walk are nothing. "I of myself can do nothing"—the mind, the body, the form, the character in the dream, the picture on the screen can do nothing. But I AM, which is All-in-all, which is without beginning and end—this *I* is Truth and can do all, because It is All.

Let each place himself in the right position. Let each know himself as he actually is. Let each behold himself like unto the Son of God, the Christed character, wherein is no separation, no division, no distinction. Life is one and Life is Totality; Truth is one and Truth is Totality; Self is one and Self is Totality. Besides this there is none else. *Believest thou this?*

Are you going to declare something about Truth, are you going to talk about Truth, or are you going to *know* Truth? Are you going to say, "Yes, I would love to study, but I am too busy; I have much that needs my attention: I must first finish the cooking and prepare for dinner; I must attend my engagements and make visits to my friends"?

How many remain from the marriage supper, remain from the eating and drinking of the river of the water of Life because they are living with the dead? "Let the dead [the dream] bury its dead," and come thou! The Master is present and calleth for thee!

Now, when you know this Truth, when you speak this Truth, you know and you speak, not because of what you have learned or studied, but because of what you are. How can we be one with Christ except we identify our Self with Christ— with "Jesus Christ in you"? Is there more than one Presence? Is there Jesus Christ *and you besides?* Are not all *one*, and is not this one *all?* When John Doe understands the nothingness of John Doe and the allness of the one Presence, Christ, then he comprehends the one perfect Man, the perfect character, Jesus Christ. You are this, I am this, there is only this—there is none else.

"How can this be?" you ask. "If Jesus Christ was Truth, as He declared, yet He was born of Mary, as the Bible states, and Truth cannot be born, what then is the explanation of the birth and death of Jesus?

"He came unto his own, and his own received him not." He came unto His own. Truth presented Itself to immortals, who were not aware of their immortality and who would not believe in Him who declared it; in Him who announced it to them; in Him who came into the dream of material existence, the dream world, to show them its nothingness.

It was not understood that the birth and the death, the coming and the going which take place in experience, is nothing. Nothing changed or happened in the spiritual world any more than if one dreamed at night that he was floundering in the deep mud and still the mud on his feet did not even soil the bedcovers!

The coming and the going of Jesus was in order that those who believed in Him and believed the Word He announced should not continue to perish in the dream, but should waken from it and know their immortality. He came unto His own, but His own received Him not. Immortals would not believe when He told them the truth; they preferred to believe in the dream. Yet God so loved the world of immortals that He sent His Word *in the flesh,* that immortals should know that the dream, unreality, is nothing; that birth, sin, sickness, and death are unrealities and that *Truth is all there is.*

When you watch the coming of a fire on the moving picture screen, when you witness the flaming of the logs, in fact, the consuming of whole houses, are you deceived? Do you rush for your life or sound the fire alarm? Not at all. You sit quietly in your seat in the theater, knowing there is no danger whatever, that nothing is happening, for those leaping flames are not even scorching the white sheet!

That which happens in the picture is nothing. It is plain to you that the fire that you see is not a fire; that when the people on the screen run with water and hose, they are not running with water and hose, nor are they extinguishing the fire.

Can you see that in the picture when they are born, they are not born? When they die, they do not die? Nothing whatever is taking place *in reality.* If you can understand this clearly and intelligently, this will be the key for you to the earth situation.

There is only heaven, wherein is no change. There is only Truth, wherein is no birth or change or death. When one is born on earth, he is not born in heaven. When one dies on earth, he does not die in heaven. If we know this, we do not run hither and thither; we are not deceived by appearances.

When Jesus was born of Mary, this was not the birth of Truth, for there was no such thing as birth in reality. Birth means beginning, and beginning means change and dying. *There is nothing besides Truth, and Truth is unborn.* There is not Christ and Jesus besides; there is not God and man besides. You cannot separate that which is *All* and that which is *indivisible.*

If we say that Christ was not born, that He was always one with God, but that Jesus was born, then we are seeing double; we are having two lives and two powers; we are seeing Truth and something besides Truth.

We express the science of Intelligence, the science that is above the mind, like this: since there is no birth and no change and no ending in Truth and since Truth is all there is and is indivisible, then what are termed birth and death are but parts of the dream and so are not actualities.

We have not two visions, one of Christ and one of Jesus. We do not thus divide Life, but we acknowledge Jesus Christ as *the only begotten* Son of God, meaning that *Jesus was the only one who entered the phenomenal world knowing its nothingness,* knowing that a dream is not anything at all, knowing that all beings are immortals in heaven.

Jesus manifested the same appearance or form as others in the dream, that is, as flesh and blood; yet he knew and announced that the flesh is nothing, Spirit is All.

Supposing, while I am dreaming in my sleep that I am weak and sick unto death, it were possible for one standing awake at my bedside to know of my dream and, in his desire to help me, to have the power to enter my dream or to impress himself upon my mind so that I could see him as part of my dream (for in no other way could he reach me in my sleep). Suppose that in my dream he comes to me and shows me that such sickness is nothing at all, that I am not actually weak and sick, but that I am actually lying quietly in my own room very harmonious, strong, and well.

If you can grasp this simile, you can understand how Jesus entered this world; how He came unto His own, and His own did not understand Him and received Him not. It would be the same as if, while I was dreaming I was sick, one came to me and told me that I was not suffering at all but that I was in my own room well and strong, and I reply, "I know better. I feel this pain. I am so weak

I can scarcely move. It is all nonsense for you to tell me that I am not here but that I am somewhere else. Can't you see I'm here, that I am suffering, and what you say about being in bed, well and strong, is just ridiculous, for we all know better.

And as He told them of their real being, of their rightful home in heaven, of the great love of God and of eternal life, they laughed him to scorn; they shook their fists at Him; they picked up stones to throw at Him; they hated him and would have killed Him *if they could.*

The idea that He should tell them that He could forgive their sins and that "repentance and remission of sins should be preached in his name ... "; that He could heal diseases, for "Satan hath bound thee"; that He could "take the sins of the whole world" into His consciousness and nothing would be added to Him—they knew better! They knew they were born in the flesh, that they were mortal beings, and that they would die. Was it not so?

It happens that when one on the couch dreams he is living in a foreign country and wishes to return to his own land, that he may take an ocean liner and after spending several days may reach his own soil. The fact is that he has never left his own home. His journey is all a false, mental creation.

So immortals who believe themselves mortals on earth and think that they must die in order to reach heaven must waken to know that they are *already* in their own country, the perfect Land.

One can never be other than what he is. No matter what he believes or thinks himself to be, man cannot change from his changeless state.

Jesus Christ came to show immortals their immortality, their true home. One can play a part, can imagine that he is a sick man or a man in great trouble; he can do this in the dream of ignorance, but he can never make it true. He can never be other than who he is.

As one enters a so-called human experience, he assumes a departure from his real home, the heavenly world; yet an assumption is not truth, and an assumption that one is a mortal being does not make one that which he cannot be; for while he plays the part of something, he is something else. If, on the stage, a young single man takes the part of a married man with a family, he assumes this part; he is seen as husband and father, still he does not deceive himself; there is always that in him which knows that it is only a make-up affair, a masquerade.

There is always that in us which knows, which remembers our real being and our real home. The part that we are now playing does not in any way deceive Self, Christ.

There is nothing needed to emancipate man except *insight*—insight to see the Truth as Truth is. There is nothing needed in a dream except to know that it is a dream and to waken to reality. In your dream you are in ignorance; you forget the real state of your daily life. In fact, such a state can be wiped entirely from your consciousness.

For instance, you may dream that you are preparing to start off on a long journey and you are to travel on foot. You are to walk miles and miles over rough and stony roads, and you dread the walk, feeling certain that you will be very weary. You entirely forget that in your garage is an eight-cylinder car! You have a car, but you have forgotten all about it; the memory of it has been entirely wiped from your mind.

Again, suppose that in your dream you are very hungry, and you walk into your kitchen for food; you are just starving for something to eat, but all the shelves are bare. You open the cakebox, hoping to find something that will stop your craving, but it is empty; yet *were you awake* you would perceive right there a delicious fresh cake that you made and placed therein that very day! Right in that very spot where you are looking is a fresh cake to greet your eye. But your eyes are holden; you do not behold what is there, and you behold what is not there.

Does this clearly illustrate to you how we can see in our daily experience what is not and fail to see what is? How we can be walking in the finished kingdom, where all about us is beauty, grandeur, abundance, and glory too wonderful to tell, yet our eyes are holden; we are blinded, asleep in ignorance, and instead of seeing the glory that is here, we behold what is not here— emptiness, sin, sickness, and death.

What is there for us to do but open our eyes to that which is? What is there for us to do but waken from the Adam-dream and take the Jesus Christ vision of perfection and immortality?

This illustration of the dream state and the waking state proves that in the "dream of material existence" we do not see what is at hand, and blinded by ignorance, we do not remember our real home and glory. As in our dream we are hungry in our own well-provisioned kitchen, looking here and there with eyes that see not, so is it not true that one can believe himself in poverty in material existence while all around him lies the abundance of heaven? That one may believe he is sick and in trouble, forced to do what he dislikes doing, yet should he open his eyes to comprehend things as they are, a different sight would greet him?

Now, if you cannot accept this fully, then accept it in part; believe it and act out your belief, saying,

"I am a perfect being now in heaven. All about me are the things that I wish and the things that I need. The discordant things that I see and do not like are impermanent, mutable, and the real things of harmony and delight are the things in which I believe and the things which I discern," and presently you *will* see them.

When sickness and sorrow and want come before your vision, remember—this is the same as looking into the cakebox in your dream; you saw it empty, while all the time one who stood at your side, awake, saw in that very place an appetizing, fresh cake; so one who is awake does not perceive cripples and beggars and invalids, but with the Christ-vision beholds only the perfect man.

This is the announcement of Truth: "There is no sick man in heaven. There is no evil in heaven." Say it and know it, for it is Truth, and because it is Truth, it is the *Word*; it is the *Power*; it is the *Presence*; it is the *Glory*.

If you say this with the fire of Spirit within you, you will feel the glow; you will feel the thrill of love and glory, and you will know.

Many times wonderful transformation scenes have taken place as, looking at what is called a picture of pain or discord or disaster, I raised my vision; I remembered the perfect land of changeless joy, and I announced, "There is no evil in heaven."

One time while in the midst of great turmoil, where all seemed confusion, pain, and trouble, I stood still, and looking right into heaven, entirely ignoring the disturbed state that seemed before me, I said aloud, "There is nothing out of order in heaven. *There is nothing out of order in heaven.*" And as I said it *because it is true*—not because I said it or thought it, but because an announcement of the Word was the Word—immediately one thing changed into another thing, one thing gave place to another thing, and the most unexpected and seemingly impossible changes took place—and lo! all was just the way it should be; all was the way it *is.*

If the reader will just try this, he will see for himself the wonders of Truth; he will see the order that can spring out of chaos, the health that can take the place of sickness, the abundance that can appear out of nothingness.

There are no miracles in Truth. It is only a transformation of sense that takes place, the losing of the false in the recognition of the true. You deliver Truth to this experience by interpreting it in accord with Truth. This is what is called *the redemption of the world.* God so loved the world that He would redeem the world, that is, we redeem the world as we redeem our experiences, as we interpret experience with ideas of Truth.

If you find it difficult to declare that you are well when you are feeling sick, then just *assume* that you are a perfect being in a perfect world, enjoying a perfect experience. *Act as though I were, and ye shall know I am.* The miracle-working radiance will take hold of you, will transform you — and you will behold *that which ought to be, is!* You yourself are the fulfillment of all that you wish, all that you desire. You cannot possibly conceive of any joy or any experience which it would be impossible for you to fulfill.

The seeing of lack where there is plenty, the seeing of sickness where there is health, the seeing of discord where there is harmony — this is a super-imposition; it is the same as while walking in the dusk, you see what is not present.

I recall walking in the dusk in my own yard a short time ago and seeing on the lawn a large black *something.* I stopped when a few feet from it, wondering, debating. It might be a dog; it might be a bear; but in the dusk I did not know. It would have been an easy thing for me to run away in fright or for me to imagine this thing coming toward me and scream for help. Had I done these things, I would have been my own victim, for in the morning I went out to investigate, and in the light I saw things as they were. The black something was only a pile of dirt.

The day before, our puppy, in order to fulfill his desire to do as he pleased, had dug a great hole in the yard and piled a quantity of soft earth around it. How differently we see in the dark, in ignorance, from the way we see in the light, in Truth! This ignorance causes a superimposition to seemingly take place, causes something to be seen which is not present; and this which is so caused is nothing, nothing at all. In the light we behold the nothingness of nothing and the fullness of reality.

So it is that we experience false imagination and false reflections because of a darkened sense, because we are asleep. As the mind becomes clear and transparent, becomes nothing of itself, it reflects the perfect understanding or perfect ideas of Intelligence; then our experience is happy and harmonious.

"I am the vine; ye are the branches." Jesus was the first immortal who understood the totality of immortality. We are to unite our vision to His vision, like the branch to the vine; we are to see as He sees, and we are to know the Self as It *is*.

Jesus announced, "I am the truth," and His birth and His life and His death and His resurrection and His absence from our sight, when viewed correctly, show that as Truth He was unborn; that He is here as much today as at any other period, for that which is, is changeless, eternal.

He redeemed the world; He brought us eternal salvation; He took upon himself the sins of the whole world with the consciousness that *man is immortal being in heaven now.*

> *Now* are My words fulfilled in your ears. *Now* heaven is here. *Now* you are healed. *Now* you have not sinned. *Now* you are the Light and the Truth. All that *I* do, *you can do,* for you are in Me and *I* am in you; and we are in the Father and the Father is in us, for we are one Self, one Being, one Totality.
>
> *I* have proved to you the nothingness of sin and of disease and even death and immortality, and you may see Me always, as *I* shall never leave you but shall always be in your midst. You may call upon My name, and *I* will hear and will answer; and you shall know that *I* am in you and shall be with you alway!

All hail! Behold our King! Behold our Truth, our heaven! Jesus Christ, the Word in the flesh, came to us in our dream of good and evil, showing us that when we are sick, we are not sick; that when we are poor, we are not poor; that when we die, we do not die; but it is "Yea, yea" and "Nay, nay," and we are what we are—*the unchanging, the unchangeable.*

We are like God—unborn, immortal, eternal—and demonstration, healing, miracle working is that man shall find himself, shall awake in his own home, his perfect land, and shall know himself *as he is* and shall know that there is nothing else but perfection!

They who believe in this miracle-working grandeur are of swift vision. They who move in the Spirit or in the Word are fleeter than they of thought; and they who believe in Jesus Christ as the Lord of this planet believe in instantaneous deliverance, believe in the plant *before* the seed, believe in the Word *before* the thought, believe in perfection *before* the healing, believe in reality, heaven, wholeness, unchangeableness here and now—man, immortal, needing neither anything added to him nor anything subtracted from him.

Experience adds nothing to you or to Life. Experience is altogether mental, and the value of experience is not for instruction or for learning, but for joy, pure joy and delight. It is when you perceive the nothingness of experience that you realize the truth about it, and this truth of its nothingness is its delight, its charm.

The nothingness of experience is not like the nothingness of void and emptiness; but its nothingness is like that of moving pictures, of a shadow or of a reflection, just as you might see your reflection in the mirror and know that though the image in the mirror is nothing, yet it is a perfect reflection of you.

The perfect world is the playground of immortals, in which they experience the ecstasy of Being.

Instruction is not to teach man. Treatment is not to heal man. To read off some notes to those whom one calls his students, as though he were thereby delivering instruction or teaching, is to be in ignorance of Truth, for Truth recognizes no student. Truth beholds no one to teach or heal. Truth knows only the real Self, who is All-knowing and perfect.

Then why speak Truth, why write Truth, why give a treatment or declare to another the facts of Life? Instruction is not to teach him, not to change his thinking, not to reconstruct him; but instruction is to remove from him the belief that he is not perfect now.

Instruction is the announcement of immortality to an immortal being, of perfection to perfect Self. Such instruction is powerful, irresistible, inevitable, for Truth compels us to be what we *are*.

We do not make Reality. It is here. We tear down the veil, the cloud, the mist by knowing its nothingness; then we behold Reality. Man's deliverance is by Intelligence, which transmits perfect ideas, perfect images. When we speak of the heavenly world, we do not mean another world off in space somewhere, but we mean that as our vision is clarified, we see the heavenly world as it is, at hand.

In the highest sense, to desire perfection or to desire a perfect experience in a perfect world is not true prayer. This is the language that we spoke at one time; yet why should one desire to be that which one already is? "Believe that ye have," said our Beloved—not *will* have, but *already* have. Does man desire food when he finds his hands filled with abundance of provisions? Does the lover desire his beloved when he feels her in his arms? What then is there for us to desire except that we become aware of all that we are?

In the absolute sense, true prayer is the rising above desire, for desire is a longing for that which one feels he has not already at hand. No matter what we wish to accomplish, it can be done, for we have the will of God to do all things. When the fire is kindled and all ablaze within us, when it consumes and swallows all that can be wiped out, then we begin to feel the love of God in our hearts, the beloved Presence with us, the ever-present Companion rejoicing with us.

Self, Soul, Spirit, I AM was never created, born, made, or produced, and all that stands between myself and Truth, being nothing, must perish.

Does one ask, "How can that which is nothing perish?" Nothing is all that can perish. That which is something is Truth and cannot perish.

Treatment is Truth spoken to Truth. Treatment is the rending of the veil. It is the burning of the chaff. It is Christ in our midst saying, "Peace, be still! Arise and come forth, thou immortal being!"

Now, there is no such one as a "mortal," and yet there is a common idea that mortals sin and must be reborn. An immortal is never a mortal; but an immortal, ignorant that he is an immortal, has been called a "mortal."

An immortal, not recognizing his immortality, is known as "mortal," and it is said that "this mortal must be reborn," that is, he who is considered a mortal must waken to the fact that *there is no such thing as a mortal being.* He must come into conscious knowledge of that which he *is,* for always one knows all things not because of what he studies or what he learns or what he feels— but because of what he is. There is no mortal in Truth, in reality, in heaven; and beside Truth, there is none else.

The Teacher is always the Self, who knows all things. You are not as much Truth as you can think; but you are all the Truth there is, regardless of what you think, for you are changeless being, always and forever. To know this is to know what is true. Truth does not depend upon your conception, your body, or upon anything whatever.

One should not be dependent upon his thinking ability, nor should he be dependent upon his mind in any way, for at that moment when he is not thinking, when the mind is not working—"Take ye no thought"—at that thoughtless moment Intelligence is present; thoughts and ideas flow over him and into him as though inherent, unattached, and he knows without any conscious effort.

Now, the mind has been called the thinking instrument. Some teachers of metaphysics have termed it a mortal mind, distinguishing this mind from Intelligence by calling the mind of Intelligence the "divine Mind." Placing a capital letter to the human instrument will never make it Intelligence, and many have tried just this, believing that the mentality could at times be divine Intelligence, while at other times it could deceive and bring about sickness and death.

To have a clear and intelligent understanding of the mind is to rest one's feet on solid ground.

The mentality is not God, is not divine Mind, is not cause. It makes neither good nor evil. Yet mind would like to announce to the world, "I am a seat of importance. I can kill with wrong thoughts, and I can heal with right thoughts. Man is according to the way I am thinking. If I am thinking evil, then man is evil; if I am thinking good, then man is good. I make the man, for it has been repeatedly uttered that man is the way I, mind, am thinking, that my thinking makes the man what he is. I put the man up or I pull the man down. Some men are afraid of me, while others worship me; some call me error and evil and devil, while others, having respect for me, call me power and intelligence— yes, and even call me God."

Now, the truth about this instrument is that it is nothing. It is nothing in this way: it is nothing as a mirror is nothing. The mind is not authority, is not intelligence, is not power, but is nothing, like a mirror. It is a reflector. The mirror presents no originality or identity of its own, but is willing to be whatever is before it; it is willing to surrender itself to the world before it. The mind is like this. Its only mission is to transmit or reflect Intelligence, true and perfect ideas.

When the mind is thoughtless, quiet, calm, it is transparent like a lake, and like a mirror with no speck of dust upon its clear surface, the mind then reflects the intelligence of Soul and images forth perfect ideas of Intelligence.

Have you not noticed many times that by taking thought you do not arrive at the desired end? Then, tired and exhausted, you relax, your mind becomes still, quiet, calm, and all of a sudden the very idea that you longed to possess is present, is right with you, in your midst, like a flash of light from the clear sky. This is true reflection, the reflection of Intelligence.

Intelligence is that which knows all and knows all as it *is*. Intelligence is not double-minded, does not choose between good and evil, does not take the right and leave the wrong. Intelligence sees all there is and sees that it is all good, that it is all just as it should be—*perfect*.

The mind is saying, "Now, I have the right thoughts to think, and if I can only hold them, they will bring the conviction to me. While the mind would say this, Intelligence, looking right over the mind, declares:

> "You are nothing. No matter what thoughts you hold, you can do nothing at all but what you are intended to do—to reflect Me, to show Me forth, to image forth My glory and My omnipotence, My wonders of perfection and My radiant joys. I, I am All, I am Spirit. I am the only Presence. I fill heaven and earth with My glories. I know that good is all there is, and besides good there is nothing else."

Intelligence is the glory of Self. The Mind of God is the Light of Intelligence, and with this Mind man beholds his glory, beholds that which he is. There is no mind to think evil. There is no mind to send forth evil ideas. There is no mind to send forth false pictures; but man by his own nature shines forth like the sun, and like the Holy Shadow, wherever he travels are those who dance with joy and shout with healing and deliverance.

You do not find understanding in books or in any teaching, for understanding is in You, Intelligence. The teaching or the reading of books brings the light to you that you may see the Presence as It is. While reading books of Spirit, do you not feel a glow of warmth, a flood of light bathing you and enveloping you in ecstasy, a sudden tenderness and abandonment taking possession of you? The book or the teaching ignited the fire. The book of Truth acts as a match setting aflame that Intelligence which you are, reflecting and radiating forth the true experience.

We hear of development and evolution, but standing on the platform of Reality, we know that what is real, what is true, what is actual cannot change, cannot be greater today than yesterday, cannot evolve, cannot unfold, for there is no progress whatever in Truth. Phenomenon can change its form and pictures and images change in outline; but nothing has thus taken place, for phenomena is not reality. You cannot become more spiritual than you now are, for the real of you is now Spirit.

Why stand still with little ideas, meager aspirations? Why live with small vision? Why be satisfied with few joys and scanty delights? If you were very, very hungry and found yourself seated at a table filled with plenty of the choicest of appetizing foods, would you pick daintily here and there, nibbling a little of this and a little of that? Not if you were very, very hungry.

We have seen those who said that they were starving for Truth. They want healing of the body and of the mind; they want a home of their own and some of the good and pleasant joys of life; yet when the food of Spirit is set before them and they are invited to dine, how do they partake?

Do they dance with joy and shout with delight when they hear that the kingdom is here already? Do they accept, "Behold, we are happy, divine, spiritual beings, perfect now and here"? Sometimes they listen with little show of attention; again, they may open a notebook and write down a few statements; but many decide that they will think it over. "We will just sit at the table which God has provided for us, and we will look over the food before we partake of it. We will be careful not to seem too hungry or to take too much."

How many of us are content with husks when we might be sitting at our Father's table, eating of the fatted calf—present abundance? When we might be dancing and singing and making merry in this universe of delight and glory?

Instead of nibbling over a morsel of food, why not, "Open your mouth wide, and I will fill it"? Is not this what the Father hath said? If you are really hungry, why not try this? Why say, "Yes, I hope to be healed some day. I know of so many others who have been; I expect to have a home of my own some day as I certainly deserve it; I am daily looking for results from my work, for I have tried so long and so hard"?

Why not open your mouth and partake of the understanding at hand, announcing, "I see the big fact. I see that I am perfectly well before I start the treatment; in fact, for me to grasp this is the treatment itself. I'll begin now, this moment, with the most glorious truth I have ever heard—that I am now a perfect being in heaven."

When you start with the highest, it is easier to put things under your feet. When you are very, very hungry and open your mouth wide, it is easier to have it filled. When you look to the mountaintops, it is easier to see things at hand.

If you want the highest, then you must stand on the absolute fact, the fact of perfection now.

Standing upon this fact, do you believe in certain physical exercises or in particular foods? Do you see advantages in special climates, baths, or circumstances? Unless you start your treatment upon the basis of your perfection and *changeless being*, your *present wholeness*, you are not starting in Truth; you are not very hungry, but are nibbling, picking here and there according to your fancy, taking up one idea and setting it aside for another that looks more attractive.

Fan the flame within you and, eating of the heavenly manna, shout, "I have attained! I am all things now!" Let your light shine, too. Be not afraid to announce words of Truth. Let Soul radiate Its glory. Hesitate not to break the bonds, to unclasp the yoke, to stand upright on your feet, knowing that you stand not alone, for you believe in Him who promised, "I will never leave you. I will be with you all the way."

"Oh, but I have tried so hard," is the cry of some. "I simply cannot get this understanding." Were Jesus speaking to you, would He not ask, "Do you believe? Do you *believe?*" He is asking this still, and it is true, as the hymn says, "All things are possible , only believe."

"Only believe, and it shall be done unto you" was our Master's promise to us. This true belief, or belief in Truth, is the door that leads to perfect understanding.

He did not say, like this, "Now, I insist that you have a clear understanding of what I am teaching.

I do not want you to blindly believe in Truth, but I want you to see clearly just what steps to take and why you take them." Ah, no! Gentle and tender was the appeal, *Only believe* ... and they who *believed* saw their sick rise from their beds and walk and their blind run and shout with unspeakable joy; they who *believed* saw their dead rise up out of their graves and walk and talk with them again in the flesh.

"But faith, belief, is blind," declare some, shaking their heads in disapproval. Yea, it is so—faith is blind! Indeed, faith is so blind that it cannot see the things which you in your egotism claim to be seeing. Faith is so blind that it sees not the pain and the trouble which you claim around you, nor does it note the fear and the trembling you mention. Yea, so blind is faith that it looks with vacant vision at the things that are seen and sees them not; and looking beyond at things which are not seen, faith beholds them, glories in them, and loves them, for *faith is the sight of God.*

Did you not know that to be blind to error is to behold Truth? What a wonderful blindness this is, is it not? Would you not love to be as blind as this? Is this not what you wish?

Have you not read in the word of Isaiah, "Who is so blind, who is so deaf as my servant? Who is blind as he that is perfect ... ?" (For the servant of

God is blind, blind to the unreal, untrue, unpresent). He who dares to close his eyes to the world of phenomena, that he may *believe* in the perfect world at hand—the world governed by perfect Intelligence, held in perfect order and wholeness, tastes of heaven.

Now, faith that is not blind is not faith. Do you know this? Faith that sees is not faith. Faith that is built on any externals, that looks where it walks, that considers and proceeds and argues and debates—this is not faith. Did not Paul know that to look at things which are seen is not faith? But to behold things which are unseen (to the senses)—this is faith, *this is the faith of God.*

Yes, real faith is blind—blind to all thinking, blind to all planning, blind to all fixing and changing. With vision fixed to the world of heaven, with heart aflame with the presence of Jesus Christ-Consciousness, man sees as he is seen and knows as he is known.

Did anyone ever understand Truth without first *believing* in Truth? No. Belief is the door. Belief is first, and after that comes understanding. Teachers have said to students, "I do not want you to believe; I want you to understand." One might as well say to a babe, "I do not want you to creep; I want you to run." It is a sure and certain thing that no one can understand Truth except he believe in Truth, except he have faith in Truth, and except he love Truth, for faith and love accompany belief.

"I do not want to *blindly* believe. I want to see," object the foolish virgins. Now, *what* do you want to see? Do you want to see where the treatment goes that one gives to another? Is it this that you want to see—how the treatment goes from the mind of one to the mind of another, whether at the top of the head or at the base of the head or just what particular modus operandi it follows?

Do you want to see how a fever is reduced, how the temperature is brought down? Or is it that you would know, when in want, just from what source the money will come—will it come in a letter from someone, or will it be found in the street, or will it not come at all, since you are unable to determine just how it would be possible?

Yes, this is what you want to see: how the waters are quieted, how the sick body takes on health, and how the dead body is raised unto life. Is it not so? If this be true, then down you are looking, right down into the sepulcher, looking for that which you will never see, never find; and no wonder your eyes grow weary and your heads become weak and your hearts turn into stones! No wonder you do not behold the blessed Master at your side, for you are not looking in His direction!

You who are looking to the body, who are looking to the mind, who are looking to mental cause and effect, to change, to unreality—look up now to the White Christ, and you will hear the still small Voice; you will feel the loving touch, and you will know the mystery of faith. You will know that faith is blind only to the dream of material and mental existence. Faith is not blind to Truth, to completion and perfection. *Believest thou this?*

Say no longer, "Pooh! Blind faith!" but take your faces from the ground and behold, this is heaven, this is joy, this is glory. The unseen is now the seen, and the heavenly is now at hand.

"But," one protests, "how can I believe I am perfect when I am so lame that I cannot take a step; when I am full of pain; when I have such evil thoughts; when I am afraid?"

Let one say, "I am perfect; there is no sick man in heaven. There is no evil in heaven." Let him say it over and over, and something will begin to burn in him. Something will begin to believe that it is true, and softly, like the breath of the morning breeze, something will whisper to him, "Yea, yea, it is so!" Then with the warmth and the fire that is burning and blazing, his belief will burst into the love of clear understanding, and he will come into intelligent discernment of God and man.

We do not come coldly to the temple of Truth. We do not come with pride of self, with conceit and self-glory, but we come with the *abandon of love;* we come *believing* in Him who "gave his life for us" that we might behold what love means, that we might behold the nothingness of all else. We come because we love Truth; we love heavenly joys; we love spiritual things. We come because we believe that there is a kingdom of joy and harmony already prepared for us, where tears and fears are wiped away, where we look into the faces of those about us and behold perfect, radiant beings.

We say Truth with love; we say Truth with faith; for it is love and faith that tell the story. It is love and faith that hasten to the marriage supper to feel the Touch, to hear the Voice, to behold the Presence, to see the Light of the world.

It is love that tells if the flame has been kindled. It is love that tells if the fire is burning. It is love that tells if the heart is overflowing.

> Come unto Me, ye who are troubled, who are weary with downward watching. Lift up your heads and look now upon the white fields. Behold, *I* give unto you peace and rest, wisdom and understanding, power and glory; for I AM THAT I AM, and *I* am the All and the Only, the One and the Totality.
>
> Come and enjoy My glory, My loveliness, My peace, My rest and My wonder.

Chapter IV

THE CHANGELESS CHRIST

All things are ours, not by attainment but by virtue of being what we are. All things are ours inherently, inevitably. This understanding of Truth is right vision.

There is no past to Truth, nor is there any future to Truth. There is no departure from or return to Truth. Truth is that which is so, that which is unchangeable and uncreated. This understanding of Truth is freedom.

Man is never subject to his mind, but mind is subject to man. When one is sick or poor or ignorant, this is a proof of what he thinks he is; but it is not a proof of what man is. Man could think himself a certain way for hundreds of years, but his thinking so could not make him so, for a thought creation is no creation, and man can be only that which he *is*.

It has been taught that if one can but harness his thoughts, he can drive them where he will, that is, if one can think long enough and hard enough, he can have experience as he wishes it to be.

The fact is, however, that when you get tangled in the web of mind, you will need something besides mind to get you out. The thing that put the yoke upon you will not remove the yoke from you, and to use one line of thought to offset another line of thought is to attempt to see through eyes that are blindfolded. No one can manage his thinking by thinking.

It is Truth that is to make you free, and Truth is the Word. The Word is not the thought. The Word springs from Intelligence, while thought has its origin in what is called the human instrument, or mental organ. Now, thought is always wanting to make a change, to modify things here and there, while Truth announces that you are *already* free, that you cannot change or be changed.

How could Truth make you free if you were not already free? If Truth freed you from evil, then there would be evil.

The allness of Truth is totality. A truth that could be made by thinking would not be Truth, for Truth is not created. Truth sets you free from evil, because there is no truth in evil. Salvation is not according to the way you think. Salvation is the grace of God, the truth of God—the truth of perfection now and here.

When one hears that he must create all things through right thinking, he should remember that all things are already done, and to perceive this fact, to recognize actuality, is to see in manifestation that which you desire. This spiritual sense is vision, discernment, the sight of Truth—Truth seeing that which is. One should thoroughly understand the distinction between *perception* and *thinking.*

"I *perceive* that thou art a prophet," declared the Samaritan woman to Christ. She did not mean that she merely thought this; she felt something deeper than this. There was something that assured her of this. To *perceive* means to become aware of through intuition. This woman was conscious that Jesus was no ordinary man, yet she probably could give no reason; but something within her told her so.

Was it not this same perception that Peter had when he exclaimed, "Thou art the Christ"? And Jesus, recognizing that Peter *felt* the truth about Him, answered, "Flesh and blood hath not revealed it unto thee, but my Father which is in heaven." Neither the body nor the mind told Peter this wonderful fact, but Soul, Spirit, made him aware of it. It is this inner awareness that is called perception, discernment, vision, or insight.

This perception may come as a voice speaking or as a guiding hand or as an impression or desire. It always carries with it assurance, for it is a state above and beyond the mind or thinking; it is a state of knowing.

Life and spiritual practice can be best under-stood through parables and stories, and we shall now consider the illustration of the snake in the rope in order to make very clear this subject of insight, perception, discernment.

We will suppose that one walks into a room which is poorly lighted, and there upon the floor, coiled in a very suggestive fashion, lies what is believed to be a snake. Fear takes hold of one at once; he is horrified and perhaps stands perfectly still, too frightened for the moment to move; or he may scream and make a hasty escape.

Supposing that one stands still and, believing that he sees a snake, desires some means of defense or some way in which to destroy this snake. Now, where is this snake? Shall one take hold of it and carry it into the yard and kill it?

Does one with insight say, "There is no real snake here; what is here is just an appearance of a snake. The belief of snake is in my mind, and I will use the weapons of this mind to destroy it. These weapons are known as right thoughts. Right thoughts can destroy this false picture or false idea in my mind, and in this way the false appearance will likewise be destroyed." Does insight speak like this?

Can we in any way or after any fashion destroy in the mind what is not in the mind? Can we destroy the belief of a snake in the mind when there is no such fact as a snake present?

You can no more destroy the erroneous belief in the mind than you can destroy the snake itself, for *both are nothing, negation.* We are to perceive the nothingness of that which is nothing. We are not to see it and then deny it; we are not to destroy it by things or thoughts. We are to have the insight which sees what *is,* and seeing this, we will also know that there is nothing else.

Suppose that one with *seeing* eyes comes into the room, and he wishes to help this one who is deceived. How shall he proceed? Shall he think something on this order: "Now, this is purely mental delusion. I must therefore create a change in this man's mind, for what he is seeing is the appearance of a false sense in his mind. If I can succeed in changing or destroying this false sense by sending him the right sense and right ideas, then he will be healed; then he will see the rope." Does this sound like discernment?

It may sound reasonable, but it is not Truth. Its foundation is ignorance, for to Truth there is nothing to change, either in the objective or in the subjective universe.

There is no false mind thinking false ideas or delusions; there is no man thinking evil or having erroneous pictures. There is only the perfect world, which is the projection or the reflection of Truth.

In this world, that which is true is known and understood, and that which is not, has no appearance whatever.

The user of the objective method would spring out to catch the snake that he imagines coiled on the floor. The user of the subjective method would leap upon the belief of snake in the man's mind. Intelligence sees nothing to destroy in the subjective world or in the objective world.

Intelligence looks above changing the object or changing the mind. Intelligence looks beyond both matter and mind and beholds the nothingness of nothing. Intelligence sees nothing to deny, but hears the blessed voice of the Beloved declaring, "I came not to destroy, but to fulfill." I came to show you the nothingness of evil and all mentality and in this way to fulfill the allness of Reality.

True treatment comes from the heart. One does not wonder whether he is saying the right words or not. One does not wonder if he is getting the syllables all right. It is the Spirit that you put into the treatment that counts. Persons have related to me wonderful demonstrations that they have brought to pass, and they have used the simplest of words, but they had the Spirit. The Spirit is the Light; the Spirit is the Fire; the Spirit is the breath of Life.

Have you ever been called upon to do some great work—perhaps someone is passing out, or there has been some accident—and as you sit by the bedside, you forget all about the one on the bed? You direct no treatment to this one. You use no words, yet you are a blaze of light. You are swept completely away from the dream experience, and for the moment, you dwell in heaven, viewing the heavenly things; and then all of a sudden something calls you back to earth. And the patient— how is he? For you have forgotten him altogether. The patient has been entirely healed.

Now, the lover does not wonder, "What shall I say to my beloved? What are the best words to use, and how can I make her understand?" As he holds her to him, he is thoughtless, yet words leap from his lips as though from a bubbling fountain, surprising even himself. And whatever words he speaks, these are the words that are sweet to his beloved, for they are living words. They are aflame with the fire of love!

It is this way when we face the heavenly Light—we receive the baptism from on High. It is the baptism of the Holy Ghost. We do not wonder then if the treatment will do the healing work. There is that within us that tells us all that we should know. There is that peace that passeth questions. It is the peace of heaven.

Thus it is that the world is not to be destroyed but is to be redeemed. Redemption is emancipation — the waking to Truth that *is*.

There is only the one Man, the perfect Character, Jesus Christ, omnipresent. A treatment is not to destroy anything or to make something disappear from the body or from the mind, but a treatment is to know reality and to know unreality. Truth never attacks evil, but Truth delivers insight which sees things as they are. Insight, discernment, correct vision is the light that shineth in darkness, seeing only the radiance of reality.

> The treatment, then, is not, "How am I to think this snake away?" but the treatment is, "Now I am to discern that *there is no snake here.*"

Aiming to get wrong belief out of the mind is as fruitless as it would be to try and take the roses out of the mirror. You cannot get out of the mind what is not in the mind. The subjective method will keep one very busy, but it will not deliver *understanding.* The removal of ideas from the mind is not the practice of Truth. Perception, with one great sweep of vision, understands that the *mentality that sees evil is nothing! The mentality that can think evil is nothing!*

The mind of God, Intelligence, sees all there is to be seen — and behold; all is perfection! All is glory! Insight does not see the snake and then deny it.

Insight beholds the rope! Insight sees that which *is—as it is.*

Do you ask, "Well, if at first I saw the snake and later saw that it was a rope, then has not a change taken place in my mind? Did not my mind change from error to truth, wrong to right, from ignorance to understanding?" No. No change took place at all, for do you know that there is no such thing as change in Reality? There is nothing in God's world that can change, and there is no other world. Is this not so? There is nothing in the invisible Truth or in the visible image and likeness of Truth that can ever be changed, for all is *changeless perfection* without start or finish.

You cannot change the snake that you see is in the rope. *Neither is it possible for you to change your mind about that which is nothing, which is non-existent.*

Understanding is not an act or an experience of the mind. Understanding is Truth Itself. The highest practice transcends all mind exhibition. In materia medica or medical practice, knives are used to cut from the body what one would not have there, and in mental practice, thoughts are used for the same end. Truth says, however, that man is perfect now and that he can have nothing added to him or anything taken from him. It is through insight, discernment, that man is delivered to Truth.

In the presence of the perfect world, we live in perfection of being and body. The highest practice is the facing of the mind toward the Light.

When we speak Truth, we do not say it as though it were a repetition of something which we learned, but we say Truth because it is as much "us" as are the hairs that are numbered on our heads, because it seems so changelessly fixed. It is easy to look at the great rocks and think how immovable they are; we could not conceive of the sky falling down upon us; we look nightly for the stars and expect to find them where we always have found them. Then shall we not follow this same conviction when we think of heavenly things? Shall we not think of man as being fixed in perfection, in love, in health and joy?

Those who believe that they are subject to ills of the flesh and the mind must see that what they need is not healing, but awakening to the fact that they are *changeless Being*. And what is more acceptable in the sight of Truth than acknowledgment? Let us acknowledge:

> "I am all good now. I am the one Life, the one Intelligence, the one and only Being now. I live in heaven, eternal joy, and peace and abundance now."

This is my acknowledgement. This is my faith. If the sick are healed, it is not because they need healing, but that God should be glorified; that they should know they have no need of healing, for they are changeless Reality."

Healing is not accomplished by healing. Healing is accomplished by knowing the Truth, by perceiving that which is, is *all* there is, and there is nothing else. Health and strength and life are not in the body, are not in the mind, but are in You, the Christ, the *only* Presence.

Truth is neither physical nor mental; Truth is that which is changeless. *I* am the Truth; the Word is Truth.

Now, you have been clearly shown how it is possible to look at one thing and in that thing see something else. This is where what is called healing is brought into play. To intelligently understand the situation, to intelligently perceive that only Truth is true, only that which is good and perfect and changeless and harmonious and complete and satisfying is true—this is the real vision, the true insight, the healing. If one is seeing other than this, if one sees something besides this, then he can know that what he is seeing is not so, is nothing.

Now, to see a thing which is not present is to be in need of the only healing there is—to be in need of insight, intelligence, right perception. You cannot heal or change or destroy that which is nothing, that which has no existence, like sickness, poverty, and sorrow. You must open your vision so that you can announce, "That which seems to be present is not present and is nothing, for Truth is all there is and there is nothing else." The knowing of this Truth is the operation of Intelligence.

Now, all the process of thought in which one might indulge would never make the snake a rope, because the rope is already a rope before one thinks it. You cannot make that which is, for it is so already; you cannot make that which is not, for it is so already. Hence, it is written, "Before they call, I will answer." Before you think you are perfect, you are perfect. Your thinking makes and unmakes nothing whatever, but *your thinking is a river of joy, a path of delight, an outlet of praise and ecstasy.*

You have heard of instantaneous healings taking place, and in most mysterious fashion, when wholly opposite means or methods have been employed. Perhaps as one kisses the feet of a dead saint, he is released, freed; or one may take a trip in an airplane and find that he is thereby healed of some disease that has hitherto been incurable. Again, a supposedly paralytic, if his house is on fire, may, without thinking, leap from his bed and run into the street as quickly as anyone else.

You may have wondered how all this can be. What is the real way of healing? What is the perfect method? The answer is, there is none. If you seek from pole to pole and from east to west, you will never find the perfect method of healing. Why? Because that for which you are looking does not exist in heaven; because man is already perfect being; because man is that which he is seeking. *Man is health.*

One may begin early to search for health. He may look to his body, and he may look to his mind, but he will not find in this way that for which he is searching. The kingdom of health is within you. You yourself are the kingdom of glory and of completeness, of dominion and power, of love and holiness—that is, your Life, your Intelligence, your Spirit, your Soul is the diamond, is the pearl of great price. You are the health for which you are looking. You are the intelligence for which you are searching.

Were you not this already, then how would you ever expect to become this? Every problem that you attempt to solve has already been solved, or else how would you ever attain the answer? The reason why you find the answer is that the answer already exists. If there were no answer already, you would never find it, but you do find it because already it is. Before you attempt the solution, the problem is solved.

This is why the man leaps from his bed and runs from his burning house, using the legs that a few moments ago he thought paralyzed—because in him is Wholeness. He has been whole all the time that he lay on the bed unable to move. Were this not a fact, he would not have had this strength and this power that sent him leaping from the bed and out into the street.

No one could ever be healed were it not that he is already healed, and the man who, having the prayer delivered to him and being full of faith, rises from the couch leaping and shouting for joy, escapes through the door of faith. His faith, his belief, is the door which opens up to him this reservoir within, delivering that sight which is already present, that health and that strength which are infinite and at hand.

> And this is the glory of God: that man shall know the Truth; that man shall know that which is and that which is not.

Health and strength and life are not in the body or in the mental organ, but are in You, are in Christ; and your mind reflects this perfection and this understanding, and your body radiates this health and glory and loveliness, not because of the mind or the body, but because of *Truth,* because of the one *Presence.*

In reality there is no process of attainment. Since there is already that perfection to which nothing can be added, a completion in which there can be no change, attainment is impossible, for attainment would be a process and would be a matter of time. If one believes that he must climb, that he must evolve and unfold from one experience to another experience, then this is what he will seem to do; but experience is not Truth, and no more relationship exists between such experience and Truth than exists between your dream in sleep and your waking hours.

It is possible to overcome the idea of progress to a great extent, so that you will not be held in the wheel of matter and mind but will have the High Vision and will look from the point of view that you have *already* arrived, that you are there *before* you start. This is deliverance from experience.

The overcoming of disease is not the overcoming of disease, for there is no such thing in the perfect world, and there is no other world. The radiant body of Truth, which everyone has in the world of Reality, is not subject to the laws of matter or mind. The world is redeemed not by changing it, but by seeing that all that is called sickness and sorrow and lack are like the snake that seems in the rope. You cannot redeem the snake. You cannot heal what does not exist.

One is emancipated as he discovers the nothingness of experience—the same as by waking from a dream. Truth is all there is, whether we perceive It or not. Truth is independent of our perception or our insight. Truth is all there is, and the perception of *Allness* and *Oneness* is the understanding of the totality of perfection, wholeness, completeness, satisfaction, peace, glory and is the single vision, is the High Watch, is the sight of God.

In Truth we find that there is always a way of escape, a way of emancipation because of the nothingness of evil. In any dream there is always the escape from the seeming danger, for if you wake and find where you really are, the danger is gone. Now, to know that the miracle-working world is right around us, nearer than hands and feet, is to find that we are in that country, that perfect land.

Have you ever heard the parable of the imprisoned parrot, the bird that was in a cage with no seeming way of escape—and the way of his emancipation? Here was this bird imprisoned in a cage whose bars he could not break, and oh, his hunger and thirst for his own land, for the tall trees in the forest, for the sparkling brook, and for his dear playmates! What bondage to be held like this, a prisoner right in the midst of his own free land.

Now, because of his wish to know himself as actually he was, one day there came to his cage a bird like himself, with fair wings outstretched as he sank to the ground at his side. The prisoner soon told his tale. He told of his longing to be free, of his great desire to toss his head in the opens air, to expose his gorgeous plumage to the glow of the morning's blaze of light, and to know that he was free to fly where he wished, to do as he pleased in this wonderworld of delight.

The sage parrot—the parrot who knew the meaning of freedom—listened attentively without a single interruption, and when the prisoner had finished his story, the bird of wisdom knew the way. He just dropped to the ground, dead. There he lay lifeless, quiet, still, while the bird in the cage stood speechless with amazement. Quickly as a wink, up flew the sage bird, off to the tall trees in the forest, disappearing out of sight.

"What a very strange thing this is," thought the encaged bird, "yet he seemed so intelligent, I thought that he would know a way for my escape. I expected him to give me some advice, to deliver a message to me; what a queer thing for him to fall down dead like that, to make believe he was dead. Yet could it be that this was a device? Could this in itself be the message for me? I do not understand it, but I can believe in it. I can *believe* that the silent message was meant for me. I will be obedient and *believe.*"

And instantly he, too, fell down dead, still and quiet at the bottom of the cage. Soon after this, his owner came along and paused at the cage. "Poor bird! He has been too cold out here, or perhaps he has eaten some poison. Poor thing!" And gently, tenderly, he picked up the quiet form and laid it under the great tree.

Then the bird understood. Then he knew the message. With leaping joy, out went his wings, and up he flew, soaring higher and higher, his joy knowing no bonds as he flew to find his deliverer whom he knew would be waiting for him.

This story teaches the lesson of belief, of obedience, and of sure deliverance. Taking the wings of faith, we fly to that Intelligence that awaits us all; that Intelligence wherein we find emancipation and unspeakable joy; *that Intelligence that is right in our midst.* Since Truth is all there is and besides which there is nothing else, then everything is free; everything is the one Life, the one Intelligence, the one Being. Faith, belief in this Message, will lead to intelligent understanding; then one enters the kingdom already prepared and at hand.

You are thinking, "How wonderful for the imprisoned bird that a brother came to him with sufficient intelligence and in such a marvelous way showed to him the way of escape." Yet did not One come to those in prison, bound hand and foot with disease—deaf, blind, lame, and even *dead*— and did He not in a most glorious and marvelous manner exhibit the way of emancipation, salvation, redemption?

What could be more stupendous, more miraculous, than that God so loved the world, so loved those who believed themselves in prison with no way of escape, that He came unto His own, came in the flesh, came eating and drinking and sleeping, that in this way He could best enter their hearts and deliver His message of emancipation?

Had He come in grand array, robed in gold and escorted by a legion of attendants, He would have been as a stranger to them. They would have been afraid to touch Him; they would have stood in awe or have run in terror. But knowing of their belief that they were bound as if in prison, with no way of escape, He came into their midst and listened to their tales of woe, and they grew to love Him—Him with gentle loving ways. They ate together at the table, placing their arms around this Beloved One and assuring Him of their belief in Him and their great love and devotion.

He told them of the way of escape, that all power lies in the Word and that the Word is Truth; that He Himself was the Word in the flesh and that, "I have come that ye might have life more abundantly ... I am come to save men's lives ... I will give My life a ransom for many." Then He explained to them that right at their very hand is the world of delight, the world for which they were searching. He told them that they were one with Him and whatever works He did, they could do as well, for the one and only power lay in each the same.

Then to show them plainly their real being, at hand, He commanded the sick to know their freedom and the blind to enjoy their seeing and even the dead to announce their emancipation and understand that Life can never die. What a wonderful thing it was to do these great and marvelous things! Yet even then many would not believe, would not show their faith in Him. These remained in their prisons.

Now, all that Jesus did was for a purpose and with a meaning. When He healed the sick, it was to present the fact that health was right there, present all the time. When He stilled the storm, it was to show them that nothing could harm them, for in them was all dominion over all seeming obstacles and difficulties. When He walked upon the water, it was to prove to them the nothingness of matter and mind.

And what about the Crucifixion? Why did He allow this to take place? Why did He allow Himself to appear to be killed and buried? What great lesson was this to embody? What meaning lay hidden in the depths of this phenomenon?

Could this Crucifixion be to show them, to objectify to them what *they themselves* must do — they who were entertaining false gods; they who were believing in many powers; they who were as in a cage imprisoned by their own beliefs? Could it be to show them that they should not believe in any power, in any intelligence, in any force greater than that power and intelligence which is within?

Could the Crucifixion be to show that all false ideas of self must be crucified? That ideas of a personal God must be crucified and as these false beliefs are set aside that man would find himself as he is, in heaven? It has been thought and taught that God was crucified, but we know that I AM never died and was never resurrected; but the gods that one worships — these gods must be crucified. When this wonderful lesson is perceived, then one understands the meaning of the Crucifixion and what it means that, "He died for us."

Jesus Christ, the High Deliverer, tasted death for every man. He entered the experience called death, knowing full well its nothingness, knowing Himself the Light of the world, and He came forth with the keys of death and hell. He demonstrated that death could not kill Him, for He was unkillable Spirit! And this is His message to us—that we are unkillable Spirit, the ever-living Life, the changeless Being.

It is the self and all that pertains to self as a separate entity that is set aside as though crucified, for as John Doe perceives that John Doe is nothing, the allness and the totality of Truth is recognized and understood. Now, this does not mean that John Doe is Truth. It means that John Doe is nothing, that Truth is *All*. This is not declaring that "I" am nothing. The only *I* there is, is I AM, and as one understands with clear vision the nothingness of self named John Doe, does he find the real Self, pure and perfect, the one Being that is *All-in-all*.

Now, the Crucifixion presents the fact that Truth cannot be killed, cannot die, cannot be hid away in the dark earth and buried out of sight. Truth is that which is "the same yesterday, today, and forever," is it not? Can this which is the same yesterday, today, and forever be crucified and killed and buried and resurrected?

The incarnation of the Supreme Being, the actual presence of Emmanuel, God with us in the flesh, was for a supreme purpose. Had man been sufficient unto himself, then God would not have been incarnated, would not have come into the world to redeem the world. If the world could have been redeemed without the coming of a Savior, then a Savior would not have come. But a Savior did come and plainly said that man must believe in Him, must take Him as the door into changeless reality. *Believest thou this?*

"In His Name" means with His power, with His character, with His love. When we speak the Word, which is that man is already saved, that man is redeemed, that man is immortal Being in heaven, we speak in His Name, we speak with His power, that is, His power is present; His glory is at hand. Thus it is that our Savior never left us, that the glory and power and dominion and peace are the same yesterday, today, and forever.

When the Voice spoke out of the clouds, many heard the words, "This is my beloved Son." Still others did not hear these words, but heard a sound like thunder. Again, when Jesus stood before Mary at the sepulcher, she saw a gardener. This again proves that a teacher was correct in her understanding when she wrote, "The heavens and earth to one human consciousness are spiritual, while to an unillumined human mind, the vision is material" (Mary Baker Eddy).

127

Some saw Jesus as Emmanuel, God with us; others saw Him as a man stirring up evil. When they saw Jesus the right way, saw Jesus as the living Christ, Emmanuel, this was not a dream, but it was actuality. When they saw Jesus other than He really was, it was simply because of the beam in their own eyes, the blur in their own vision.

Those who weep when they mention the Crucifixion, those who mourn over the suffering of Jesus, those who meditate about His death, such as these must awake and shout for joy; such as these must see the wonder-lesson, must grasp the deep significance, must know the mystery of love, overshining all. To contemplate this love that Jesus had for the world is to feel with the heart that depth of joy and praise which is unspeakable.

To know that an immortal cannot die, cannot be other than what he eternally is, and all that testifies not to the glory of God and the omnipresence of goodness is without fact or reality is the vision of emancipation, the miracle-working redemption, the tasting of heaven.

There is no way of the mind through which deliverance can be obtained; no method in which one can acquire perfection; no way to think in order that healing come to you; no idea to hold that will free you. There is but one way of deliverance, of redemption—this is through insight. Were it true that as a man thinketh so is he, then man would be the creator of Truth, and in order to have Truth, he would first have to make or create It with his thinking.

Perception is not the creating or the changing or the adjusting of anything at all, but perception is *the abolition of all mind and all mind-processes.* Instead of removing ideas from the mind, one knows that they have never been there. Instead of creating right ideas through mental activity, one recognizes that Truth is now all there is; that this Truth is changeless, omnipresent, and is now in manifestation.

Man has dominion over his thinking, and this dominion does not consist in war. It is not the battle of thoughts, not mind over mind, for the man who cleans his house or mental home this way will but discover other stronger devils continually entering it.

> "When the unclean spirit is gone out of a man, he walketh through dry places, seeking rest and finding none; then he taketh with himself seven other spirits more wicked than himself, and they enter in and dwell there; and the last state of that man is worse than the first."

There is no battle in heaven, no force of will or mind. It is neither by might nor by power, but by

My Spirit, My Presence. Dominion consists in recognizing Reality, in knowing that which is, and in perceiving the nothingness of nothing. You have dominion over your thinking through Intelligence. While thought is constantly changing, Intelligence remains the same. You have power over your thoughts by virtue of your being. Such power is inherent in you. Power is not in thought, but power is in You. "Behold, I give unto you power to tread upon serpents [evil beliefs], and nothing shall by any means hurt you." The ability to understand the nothingness of matter and mind is the basis of escape, of emancipation.

Behold, I give unto you power! This power is already ours. This power is our being. Let us have faith; let us believe in the Word, for the Word is Truth. If one feels the need of faith or feels the desire for quickening, then let him place himself in the presence of one who has it. If one wishes to increase his faith, let him listen to one who has faith, for if one has faith, he can stir faith in others, as all have it in reality. It is inherent the same as life, and by your contact with another who has this fire of faith burning within him, faith in you will be awakened, stirred into being. Thus faith can be cultivated by instruction and by contact with a teacher of Truth, and it can be flamed into a living presence by love, praise, and devotion.

The Word is not made up of sounds, nor is it a composition of right ideas, *but the Word is the living Truth.* Therefore, do not speak the Word and expect a result. Speak the Word because it is true, for the Word Itself is the realization and is simultaneous with Its embodiment. One must always know in demonstration or in treatment that nothing whatever is taking place, nothing is changing, nothing is being done, since all is perfect *now.*

There is no material being; there is no mental being; there is no personal being; there is no appearance of any such being. There is only the being of Truth, which is neither of the mind nor of the body.

Why did Jesus say that He came to save sinners, if there is no sin? And why His prayer, "Deliver us from evil," if there is no evil from which we must be delivered?

If there were evil, it could not be removed, for whatever there is, is Truth, as Truth is all there is; besides Me there is not anything else. That which is true is reality; this is all that exists, and this reality is changeless.

The only reason why you can be delivered from anything is that such a thing is unreal.

Escape from evil is perception, insight, understanding and is not a mental process or mental action. Escape from evil is the awareness, through

Intelligence, of the truth of Being. It is Truth knowing Itself. By destroying evil you do not destroy anything, for if you could actually destroy evil, you would be making a change. You would be creating a change, whereas there is no change in Truth. True instruction is an Announcement, a Message; it is the speaking of the Word, the hearing of the Word, the eating and the drinking of divine Substance.

If you thought of a pile of dirt on the ground as a bear, and I said to you, "That is not a bear," would I have changed the dirt, or would I have removed the bear? No. Not at all. No change would take place. You may say, "But the idea of the bear was removed from my mind."

No. It was not. Nothing took place in the mind. If, in his delusion, a man sees his house afire, you do not send out fire engines, do you? And when he sees his house as it is, it was not because the wrong idea was taken out of his mind and carried off, was it?

In the highest practice we do not change our minds. Yet how many millions of people today are trying to effect a change in their minds—a change that will bring about a corresponding change in their world? How many are there using mind-changing, believing that this is the way of Truth? They believe that if they can only change their minds,

then all will be well; then their world will be a
better and a brighter place in which to live. Now,
this is no reflection upon right thinking, not at all,
for it is right and good to have right thoughts; but
we are considering the highest practice.

To change our thinking in order that we may
thereby create a change in the world is not the
vision of Truth. No change needs to take place in
the world any more than a change was needed to
take place in the dirt. The world does not need to
be changed. You do not have to put out the flames
to the man's burning house. We do not have to get
rid of evil or to war with sin, disease, or sorrow. If
we think that we do, then we are trying to kill the
bear; we are seeing the snake instead of the rope.

It has been taught that since the false idea is in
the mind, a change must take place in the mind,
which would be wholly a mental process, a warfare
in the mind—mind-changing. But changing your
mind will never change the world. The redemption
of the world consists not in the destruction of evil
or in mind-changing. Truth announces that there
is *only* Truth, and Truth is *all* there is, and besides
Me there is not anything else.

Perception says that you do not change the
thoughts in your mind. Perception does not remove
ideas from the mind or change them, but *perception*

announces such ideas are not there. They do not have to change; they have never been there.

In the mental or subjective method you heal by "taking thought." You consider the wrong thoughts in your mind and attempt to change them or cause them to disappear by the presence of other better thoughts. But thought is not a healer. *Truth is the only healer, and Truth heals by delivering man to Truth.* The understanding of Truth is not thought, but is Truth. The science of Intelligence is not the practice of mind-changing, but is an utter renunciation of the mind!

If you are sick today and well tomorrow, no change has taken place. You could never find the pain that left, could you? Have you ever discovered the place of darkness when light is present? When you see the rope today where yesterday you saw the snake, whither has your ignorance gone? Now, the coming and the going of ignorance and darkness, or any wrong idea whatever, is nothing. There is no operation that takes place; there is no process whatever.

You can think millions of thoughts, and yet nothing is happening to the mind. You can place a million different objects before the mirror, and yet when they come and go in the mirror nothing has taken place. You do not have to take one object out of the mirror before you can put another one there.

When the cat moves out of the mirror and the dog arrives to view himself, no change whatever has taken place in the mirror. The cat did not change into the dog, nor was the cat removed so that the dog could take its place; and the mirror is exactly the same when they are reflected in it as after they leave it.

Nor do you take the mirror to the shop and get it repaired when the dog leaves it. You do not have to wash it or dust it so that the cat may be reflected in it, for in their coming and going no action has taken place; no change occurred.

It is the same when thoughts of sickness and sin and trouble come and go in the mind. As the mirror does not change when it reflects first some flowers and then some children, so the mind undergoes no change when it thinks, reflects, one way and then another way. The mirror does not change and the reflection in it is nothing; likewise the mind changes not, and the ideas of sin and sickness are nothing.

The world of changeless Reality is all there is. Man is an immortal being in heaven now. Man is changeless Reality.

You do not make yourself or unmake yourself. Truth establishes you and holds you forever what you are. Rise, then, in your own name, which is His name, for there is none other name whereby you shall know emancipation.

In His Name, the name of Truth, behold yourself as you are, perceive Truth as Truth is; then will you find yourself in the land of peace and wholeness and in the world of joy and delight.

Chapter V

"No Condemnation"

There is a certain charm about right instruction. One knows as he partakes of it that it is Truth. When one finds himself in what seems a difficult position, he needs this right instruction. The moment has arrived in his experience when he must know—when Truth says, "You shall know Me, from the least to the greatest."

The science of Intelligence delivers to man what is already within him; this is why it comes with charm and joy. Man finds himself.

Intelligence delivers to one the knowledge of himself. As Truth is indivisible, and besides Truth there is not anything else, Truth is One and Truth is Totality. This, then, is the basis upon which one sets his feet: *There is no evil in Totality*, for all is good. To intelligently perceive and know this and to know why it is true is to find satisfaction, joy, and glory.

The questions you must ask yourself are: Am I going to believe in anything besides God? Am I strong enough in understanding so that I can stand in the midst of what is called discord and confusion and can announce, "It is not so! There is no such thing present!"?

137

Am I going to know that there is never any-thing for me to treat? I do not treat the body; I do not treat the mind; I do not treat wrong beliefs; I do not treat a person; I do not treat wrong appearance. I am to perceive that Truth, good, wholeness, perfection, completeness is *all* there is, omnipresent, and what is called evil is nothing.

Do I actually understand that appearance of evil is nothing, and do I understand why it is nothing? Do I understand that wrong thoughts in the mind are as much nothing as are wrong appearances?

When one looks at a rope and sees instead a snake, this appearance of a snake is nothing; conse-quently, the belief in the mind is nothing, for a belief about nothing must also be nothing.

Now, this is a very important point to clearly understand—that the false belief in the mind is nothing, and its false appearance to that mind is nothing.

Therefore, we do not treat this *nothing*, either in the mentality or in the external, but we do perceive its nothingness.

When one walks away from the mirror, his reflection also disappears. You will note that when the reflection disappears, no hole is left in the mirror, as though something had come and gone. Nothing whatever has taken place; its coming and going was no act whatever. All that keeps your reflection in the mirror is the fact that you are standing before it, and all that brings about what is called disease and evil in the universe is the belief that Truth is not all there is, but that there is something else besides Truth.

As one stands before a mirror and sees himself reflected therein, likewise one holds wrong thoughts and beliefs and sees them reflected before him. As one walks away from the mirror, his reflection also disappears; likewise, when one intelligently perceives the nothingness of both matter and mind (for this is all that seems to cut man off from the Truth which he is), that instant the disease or trouble vanishes.

Health, harmony, perfection in manifestation is true reflection of God, the reflection of Truth, and it is this reflection that is called the perfect world.

When Soul asks of the heart, "Where art thou?" what is your reply? Do you say, "Oh, I feel so wretched. I see evil as evil, and I constantly watch for the trouble to disappear. I watch the body to see if the change I am desiring is taking place there, and I watch the mind to see what thoughts I am holding"?

When Soul asks of the heart, "Where art thou?" do you reply, "I am with Thee"? Do you say, "I behold

Thou art *all* presence, *all* power, and *all* reality, and besides Thee there is nothing else whatever"?

And Soul returns, "Blessed art thou, for neither matter nor mind has revealed this unto you, but eternal Truth has claimed Its own!"

We are to know that the kingdom of glory is here, and we are this kingdom of glory. We are to know that man cannot be ignorant, cannot have evil thoughts, cannot create evil appearance. Man is like God, and we make no separation or distinction whatever. We are to know that Jesus Christ was seen in the picture-world that man should behold himself, that man should see himself as he is, that man should know that there is only one man and this man is Totality.

As you look over the universe, you may exclaim, "How can there be only one man when I see an infinite number of men? How can man be one and be infinite in number?"

You can accept that there is only one 2, yet looking through a book of arithmetic, you will see hundreds of 2's, will you not? You can see that although there is only one 2, yet you see in the visible world an infinite number 2's.

It is so with man. *Multiplicity is in the reflection.* The infinite number is in phenomena, and this does not contradict or deny unity. You are one person, yet you might stand in a room where there were fifty mirrors arranged about you, and you would see fifty forms like your own. One should clearly see and comprehend this point, for it is a most valuable one and very necessary to understand in demonstration.

There is but one Life, one Intelligence, one Consciousness, one Being, one Man, and this oneness is Totality. This Totality is indivisible, that is, It is not divided into parts or particles. Now, you can have all the air there is to breathe, and I can have all the air there is, and still the air will not be depleted; nothing will have happened to it. Your taking the air will not cause a separation to take place. You can have all the understanding of mathematics, and I can have all the understanding of mathematics, and your understanding will then be my understanding. There will be no difference whatever. You cannot separate that which is one, and that which is one is all.

An illustration of great clearness is to consider a lake, over which is a sheet of ice. Now, into this ice has been cut many holes as forms of circles or squares or figures of different sizes and shapes. Can you see that though the forms are many and varied that under each one is *the whole lake.* There is not a little bit of water under this hole and another bit of water under that hole, but under each, regardless of its shape or outline, under each is the whole body of water. So back of each one called man is the whole Life, the totality of Intelligence and Power, *infinite Being.*

If in one place the ice has been cut to make a queer and unattractive-looking figure or form, it matters not; the lake is just the same under that place as it is where a beautiful form has been cut.

There is but one man, and whenever you see man, you see this one man, for there is none other. If you see a cripple, you are seeing what is not there, the same as you might see the bear where there is a pile of dirt. There is only perfect man, for there is only perfect Truth, and there is none else.

It will help you, when you feel that you are seeing disease and evil, to stand still and say:

"No, I do not see this, for it is not present. The perfect man is all there is here, and this perfect man is here whether I see him with my physical eyes or not. With my spiritual vision, with my Soul intelligence, I know that he is here and that he is perfect."

This is the way you are to redeem your world — by setting aside the false vision as nothing, not through denial, but through intelligent understanding. You are to behold the nothingness of nothing, and you are to announce the oneness, the changelessness, *the totality of Truth and Truth's perfect reflection.*

Thus, the perfect world, heaven, the kingdom of glory is at hand and coexists with God, Truth.

It is the mind that is causative; thus, it is said that all causation is mental. Yes, but it must be clearly understood that all such mental creation is the same as that of the pictures shown on the motion picture screen. Such creation comes and goes, for such creation is not Truth's reflection, but is *mind's creation.* All that does not measure up to changeless perfection, completion, harmony is not Truth, hence is nothing.

Truth is *all* there is, and this is final. We are not to say, "Yes, of course, I know that in reality Truth is all there is, but here is also this other, and what are we going to do with it? How shall we attack it so that it will disappear? What action must we take that we can bring out the true reflection that exists?"

We are to look at what is called "this other," and with the understanding that we had delivered to us we are to say, "It is not so! It is not here! Truth is here, and Truth is all that is here!" Then what has been called the action of heaven takes place—we behold our world as it is.

Now, Jesus did not lose or suspend His true being when He was seen as a man walking on the earth. He was never less than God, Truth, at any time, and his mission was to bring emancipation to those who would accept. It is written that for several centuries after Jesus' ascension, it was quite universally taught and accepted that Jesus was the Messiah, the Christ, promised to the world and that great healing took place "In His Name."

Gradually this understanding of Jesus began to change, and the mind conceived the idea that Jesus was only a man such as other men, except that He was very wonderful and seemed to possess superhuman power and glory. As the belief that Jesus was God changed to the belief that Jesus was man, so also a change came in the healing works, and less and less spiritual healing took place until, after many centuries, it quite passed out of view.

Now, Jesus was both perfect God and perfect man—the Son of God and the Son of man. When instructing His disciples, we hear Him at one time speaking of His Godhood, and again we hear Him speaking of Himself as man. Right here is where metaphysicians have divided Jesus Christ. They have termed His Godhood "Christ" and His manhood "Jesus." But why make this separation and distinction? You cannot divide or separate Life, can you?

In the transfiguration, Jesus transcended matter, and His body was radiant as the sun and as bright as the light, so that one could not continue to look upon Him for the greatness of His glory. Jesus

Christ was one being, the same being when He lay in the manger as when He ascended on high. His appearance to a world blinded with ignorance, whether as babe, man, or king, did not in any way change Him. Being cannot change; Life cannot change; Reality cannot change.

Jesus as Deity was not born and did not "suffer and die," but as "the son of man" He did. Yet, as man, He proved their *nothingness* that we might do likewise. He said:

> "I came not to destroy the mental world but to redeem you, to emancipate you from belief in any world except the world of love and harmony, the heavenly world of reality which is at hand and within you. Although I appeared in this world as a babe born of Mary, I explained that, "Before Abraham ... I Am—that I was with the Father before the world began.
>
> "I came to show you the nothingness of nothing and the allness of Truth. I came to show you the power and the glory and the might and the majesty that lie within you. I showed you the nothingness of blindness and deafness and all manner of diseases; I showed you the nothingness of material laws and of mental laws. I placed this proof right before your eyes, and you saw redemption, restoration, and emancipation take place.
>
> "Now go and do likewise! Redeem your world with the vision that I have given you. Redeem your world by knowing that evil is not something to be destroyed, but evil is to be seen

as deception. Then shall you walk in the finished Kingdom, in the City of Righteousness; then shall you waken in the perfect world, having My name in your forehead, the name Jesus Christ, I Am.

"There is no condemnation to rest upon you. I have overcome the world. You are the light of the world—free, flawless, and victorious! *The works that I do, ye shall do also. Preach the gospel; heal the sick; raise the dead, and, verily, I am with thee alway!*"

I am reminded of my first experience in receiving healing. It was given me by a Christian Science practitioner over twenty years ago. All I knew about the subject at this time was that it had healed my mother, father, and sister. The healing in each case was almost instantaneous, that is, only a short time elapsed between the first treatment and the healing.

Now, in those early days of spiritual healing, no practitioner ever spoke of a case as being difficult or as taking time or that there were certain thoughts to be changed before the healing could be manifested. It was presented to us in those days that the idea of sickness is a *deception;* that man, the image of God, could never be sick; that when one seemed sick, he was actually perfectly well; that when it looked as though lungs had wasted away, that in reality they were present, just as they should be; that evil of any name or nature was purely a deception, an unreality or hallucination, and all that one had to do was to know that man is perfect now and that there is nothing to heal.

This was the early presentation of Christian Science; but every mind would set up something for itself, and it seems that this wonderful, clear presentation and conception of the omnipresence of perfect Being and the nothingness of evil has gradually faded away, to some extent, so that many do not now view the temple of Truth like this but look rather to their own minds for guidance, direction, healing, and power.

Now, the first treatment I ever had for a physical trouble was while I was visiting a friend who was a Christian Science practitioner and who saw the temple of Truth with this clear, right vision. While with her one day, I was seized with great pain which seemed to fill my whole body. As I walked the floor wringing my hands, she said to me, in her gentle way, "Come, lie on the sofa here, and I will help you."

Now, I thought that I could not do this, for I could not stand still or sit still, and I recall that I was somewhat provoked that she should take the matter so lightly and not realize how very much I was suffering. "I will do what you ask," I replied, "but you will see that I will not be able to stay quiet."

As I lay on the couch, this practitioner sat in a chair by my side, and opening a small black book at random, she read these words aloud, "Let God be true, and every [material] man a liar." These words were quite new to me, and they surprised me a great deal, for at that time I did not understand their meaning. I watched, as immediately she closed the book and closed her eyes, and do you believe it?—that was all I knew.

It was just as if there had been some figures on a blackboard and someone came along and with one sweep of his hand erased them. Something came over me that *instantaneously* erased all before me. The next thing I knew, I opened my eyes to find out that I was alone and had been asleep for over an hour. I found a note pinned to the pillow telling me at what time my friend would return home.

How was this, that at one moment I could be suffering with great pain, and the very next instant I could be quietly, calmly sleeping? Could it be other than that I was perfectly well *before* I lay on the couch? True healing is instantaneous, because true healing and true being are the same, are one, and this is changeless reality; hence, healing is not dependent upon time. The treatment is the healing; the vision of reality is all there is to know.

If the pain went out of my body, I certainly was not aware of it, for when I wakened there was no consciousness of a vacancy any place, as though something had been taken away or had moved out; and if the pain went out of my mind, it did not leave any cavity. I did not feel that my thoughts had been moved around and were in different places, as one might enter another's house and rearrange his furniture. I only knew that I was fine, feeling radiant and as free as the air.

Such is true treatment and healing—to know yourself as you are, to be undeceived, to be demesmerized, to see the rope a rope. As one would not call in his neighbors to locate the snake after he had perceived the rope, so one does not wonder where the pain goes when he feels his health and strength and glory.

It must be understood that man is just as perfect when what is called disease is imaged forth, as when what is called health is imaged forth; he is just as perfect, for *he is a changeless being.* The white screen does not change, whether a fire is raging on it or a dam has burst its boundaries. The screen is just the same; the fire and the water never touch it.

149

It makes no difference to Truth whether you view it as Truth or as evil. Truth is Truth, nevertheless, and is all there is, and even while you feel sick or lame or sinful, still, at that very instant, you are only one way—*you are perfect immortal being,* and what you call sickness and sinfulness never touch real being. Can you grasp this deep fact of Life? This is the vision that rends the veil. This is the vision that causes one to leap from his bed and refuse any longer to be in prison, *for what prison can hold a spirited being!*

A mortal should never claim that he is God, for he is not; yet do we not frequently hear of this being done? If one does not have the insight to know the nothingness of matter and mind, he is termed a "mortal," which means that he has yet to waken to the Truth of Being, and, in this state of ignorance, for him to claim that he is Christ or God would be a falsity.

This is where many have fallen from the path. This is where many are not viewing the temple of Truth as it is. Much confusion and discord have been manifested in the field because of the teaching that the mind or mentality is God and that each should claim for himself that he is Omnipotence. Now, for one believing in the reality of the mind to claim himself to be God would be like darkness claiming to be light. There is no darkness; all is light. There are no mortals; all are immortal beings. *But one must know this,* and until he *does* recognize this great and wonderful fact of being, then let him "watch and pray that he be not led into temptation."

As one enters the light, he naturally and laborlessly perceives things as they are and does not call ignorance understanding; does not call black white or darkness light. One with insight, divine illumination, knows that John Doe, ignorant of the nothingness of matter and mind and appearing in the picture as sick or lame or blind, cannot go among his brethren proclaiming, "I am God," and succeed in this deception.

Naturally, the layman asks, "Since you are God, then why do you not demonstrate it? Why not do the works that Jesus did?" As the darkness is nothing, as ignorance is nothing, so a mortal is nothing, and *one must spiritually discern the nothingness of mortality before he lay claim to a higher light.*

When John Doe, with divine illumination, perceives the nothingness of John Doe and knows the one name—*Jesus Christ,* Truth, God—to be the only name there is in heaven and in earth, then he speaks as the Spirit directs; then he is aware of his immortality.

When Jesus said, "Rise and walk," He was not addressing a lame man. While others were viewing a weak, sickly man who was unable to stand upon his feet since he was born, Jesus did not see things this way.

It would be the same as though a delirious person were looking at his nurse, and suddenly he sees her as a great giantess wearing a tall, black hat and a great, black coat. Another in the room, with right vision, sees a small, pleasant-looking woman wearing a white cap and dress.

The sick man's creation is altogether mental, that is, he is making it himself with his mind; hence, being mental, it is nothing. If those around Jesus saw a cripple, they were looking at mental creation, creation other than the reflection of Truth, while Jesus saw the kingdom the way it is.

Jesus had the right vision. He knew there is only one world, peopled with immortal beings who leap with joy, and with this vision *before* Him, He told the man to rise and walk, for, of course, a perfect man can do this. *He spoke to the perfect man. He commanded the strong, well man to do that which can be done. He saw what He knew there is to be seen!*

Wrong belief is nothing and can do nothing!

This is the announcement of Truth, of right vision. One does not look upon fear, ignorance, wrong thinking as evil, but perceives them as nothing. This is what takes the sting out of the serpent. When you know a thing is nothing, you are not afraid of it;

you are no longer a slave, held in prison by an
illegal sentence pronounced upon you.

Fear, ignorance, wrong thinking has no foundation whatever. You can understand that 3 and 3
are 6, whether you are thinking it or not and
whether you know it or not. *Your thinking and your
knowing have nothing whatever to do with the fact
itself.* While you are believing that 3 and 3 are 5,
this wrong thinking does not make any change
anywhere; and while you are knowing that 3 and
3 are 6, neither does this bring about any effect.

Your thinking, then, either wrong or right,
has nothing to do with the fact itself.

Truth is self-existent and is in no way dependent
upon our thinking. The notion that one must operate
Truth or set it in motion or bring it out into manifestation is altogether an ignorance.

Truth is now perfect in the unseen, and
Truth is now perfect in the seen.

There is nothing to bring out that has not been
brought out; there is nothing to do that has not been
done. What we must do is *look and behold, perceive and
understand.*

Man must ever be the way that he is; he cannot
be otherwise. He does not have to be made, nor
does he have to be unmade. One can never get rid
of 2 and 2 are 5, and one can never get rid of evil.

When one sees reality as it is, nothing has been lost or taken away from him. In losing ignorance, he does not lose any part of himself. When one loses the idea that 2 and 2 are 5, he is not conscious of anything being taken away from him.

There must be no compromise. In the perfect practice, in the science of Omnipotence, one does not sense evil away or attempt through thought application to change its form or location. It is just as unavailable and unlearned to do this as it would be ridiculous and totally without sense to look at the snake that is seen in the rope, and in order to get rid of it and to get it out of the mind, one sense the snake as moving across the floor and depositing itself under the radiator.

Now, as long as one believes he has put the snake under the radiator, it is apt to come forth at any moment, and as long as one looks at disease and senses it changing from one form to another, from one place to another, just so long is he putting a ball and chain on his ankles; for when the snake comes from its hiding place, the victim will he more frightened than ever, and when the disease that has been sensed from a swelling state into a discharging state breaks out in another form, one is more fearful than ever. Thus, man is tied with the shackles that he made himself and, knowing not that he is in ignorance, gropes around in the dark.

One teacher clearly stated, "Mortal mind is subject to any form of belief." That is, one using his own mind as power, one believing in mind as creator, becomes his own victim. In your dream at night, if you are falling off a precipice, it is you who made that precipice. You placed yourself in this dangerous position, and, should you fall, you are your own victim.

Why remain in the darkness of ignorance when the light is once clearly presented to you? As long as one believes in his own mental creative powers, just so long is he victimizing himself, just so long is he making the blindfold that he places on his own eyes. Intoxicated with his own ignorance, he must at some time reach out for the true Light.

In the science of Intelligence one does not labor with mental creations; one does not manipulate thought; one does not see how pain escapes from the mind or body. Divine science is not mind over mind, nor is it mind over matter or body. Be sure you understand this great and important point — that the science of Intelligence, the perfect practice, is not a battle of minds, nor is it the practice of dominion over matter.

This is understanding indeed, like a burst of glorious light, for many have been taught and have accepted as true practice that one mind may be stronger than another mind and that the stronger is the winner.

In the glorious light of insight, one with a great sweep of intelligence now puts both mind and matter out of consideration and announces that what is termed *matter* is mind, and what is termed *mind* is nothing. Do you not feel the ecstasy of inspiration, the fire of illumination, as such a blaze of light strikes your Soul?

You think of yourself as perfect Intelligence — not your mind as Intelligence, but your *Self,* your *Soul,* your *I* as Intelligence — and you think of your mind as a perfect reflector or perfect mirror projecting that Intelligence which You are.

You think of your body, not as matter governed by certain thoughts that you or the practitioner is thinking, but as the perfect reflection of Truth. Your body is then controlled by Truth — not by your thinking or by the thoughts of anyone else, but by Truth. You think of yourself as Spirit, Love, I Am, radiating joy and peace and wholeness and power, and this as being reflected by your mind and body into all your affairs. Thus, we have Intelligence and Its image and likeness, God and His manifestation as *all there is.*

When illumination lights your consciousness, it breaks forth like a burning flame into all your affairs. We have been taught to say, "My business is a success. My business succeeds and prospers," but with insight, we no longer work for a successful business after this fashion, for this would be casting down our vision. It would be looking at the image and attempting to control it by certain means of the mind.

With insight, we announce, "I *am* success," for it is *Self* that is the success and not the business. Is this clear to you? When you know who you are and why you are, then you know yourself as you are known, and you understand intelligently that because of your *being*, you are *inherently* a success, and it is said of you, "All that thou doest shall prosper."

This is the heavenly message. This is the message of the super-world—that emancipation, touching you, will enter into all your affairs, and wherever you walk, success goes before you. When divine illumination strikes you, it strikes into all that you do; it reaches here and there and all over, and "Whatsoever thou doest, it shall prosper."

Now, insight is as though there were a great lake that must be emptied, and one comes with a thimble; and day after day and year after year, he toils away with this thimble in order to empty the water from the lake. Another comes with a pail, and year after year he continues to empty out the water from the lake with this pail. But one day one with insight, an illumined being, walks by, and seeing that the lake must be emptied, with one sweep of his hand over the lake, the water entirely disappears, and only the dry earth is seen. He knows how to accomplish within the instant what another would never accomplish even in a hundred years.

It is the same as this with healing. One comes along, and, seeing a body that needs to be healed, a mind that needs to be emptied of disease, he sets about with certain thoughts to empty out of the mind of this individual his wrong thinking; and day after day and year after year, he keeps on using his own thoughts to empty the mind of another in order to clear out the diseases which he believes abide there.

Then one day there comes an illumined being who, with one grand sweep of insight, discerns that *man does not need to be emptied, that no disease abides in him at all,* and he commands, "Rise and come forth," and he who is bound with the beliefs of matter and mind finds himself where he always was—in the world of heaven.

Now, one can nibble here and nibble there and experiment with this idea and that idea and with one system or method and then with another, carrying a newer trademark to catch the eye of the mentality; but the man of Intelligence knows what he knows, and he announces that matter and mind are both nothing, that Truth is neither one nor the other, and that Truth is Totality, or all there is. With this daring Intelligence, he with one swallow swallows up the whole belief in evil, for what evil is there in belief outside the body and the mind? Has there ever been found a place to locate evil except in the world of matter or in the world of mind?

And so when you once clearly and intelligently perceive that evil is neither in the body nor in the mind, then you have the insight that perceives the nothingness of evil, and it is said that to perceive the nothingness of evil is to live in a world of charm and glory.

Reality exists above mentality. This is no reproach upon right thinking, not at all; it is right to have right thoughts, but in the practice of Understanding, we place things in their proper position. It is as though one has handed to him a great puzzle picture, and all these small pieces of cardboard must each be placed in the right position to insure a perfect and complete picture. Now, we must place the puzzle together so that each idea is fitted into its proper place. It is right to have ideals, expectations, right thoughts, and ambitions, but only in placing each where each belongs does the perfect picture stand before our vision.

One cannot count upon material things to furnish enjoyment such as will completely satisfy; neither can one count upon mental thinking to completely quench one's hunger and thirst for spiritual peace and blessedness. If one has no matter, no time, no space, no evil, no cause or effect, no opposites, then he demonstrates. It is said by the illumined that it is then the same as though one had an empty blackboard before him, a board upon which nothing is written—he can write as he will. He has entered the open door.

It seems hard for one trained in mind power, seeing another in pain and trouble, not to attempt to do something with his own mind in order to help. It is the same to him as if he saw a house afire, and, wanting to help, he runs for a pail of water to throw upon the flames; so when he sees suffering, he rushes to his mentality for sentences to pour over the mind of the sufferer; yet this is not the way of Truth.

Truth does no work. *Truth knows.* One must at such times merely let his light shine. That which is true does not change from better to worse or from worse to better, and one is to know *changeless being.* Instead of going to the mind for instruction, as a student might approach his teacher for knowledge, *you* are the instructor *yourself,* and you are to speak to your mind living words, teaching the mind, "I am the power of the Truth." Always know that *you are the teacher of your mind,* that your mind comes to you for orders, that your mind must be obedient to *you*, and that you are not at the mercy of your mind.

In the East this subject is considered as a man driving a chariot. The driver is man, Intelligence; the reins, the mind which guides and directs the horses, or senses; the chariot is the body; and the road is the world over which he travels. Now, should the reins drive the horses and keep them under control without any man upon the seat in the chariot, it would then be the same as when the mind, without Intelligence to guide it, attempts to control the body and its affairs. With Intelligence to teach and guide the mind and the senses, the body is kept in safety, and one has a harmonious experience.

There are millions of people attempting to control their bodies and their affairs through their minds; and is it any wonder that we witness today such a great confusion, such a running hither and thither and falling into ditches? As long as one looks to his mind for instruction and help, he is in ignorance.

When one understands that Intelligence is not in the body or in the mind but is *above both*, that Intelligence is *I*, or Self, then he has knowledge, understanding.

It is written, "There is therefore now no condemnation to those who are in Christ Jesus." You who have ignorantly bound yourself to a bed of sickness are believing that your thoughts have placed you there, are you not? You who are believing this falsity are admitting condemnation as a power to hold you down.

Rise now, and with eyes toward the Light and with face toward the heavenly City, announce:

> There is now no condemnation to those who are in Christ Jesus! There is now no condemnation upon me! I am not condemned to pain and ignorance through wrong thinking! *I am free!* The Spirit of Truth sets me free from the law of condemnation for, "Ye are not in the flesh but in the Spirit, if so be that the Spirit of God dwell in you. "

When you declare a thing, you do so because it is so. When you say, "I am free now," you say this because it is *true,* because it is the *Word;* but should you say, "I am free now; I am well; I am strong;" — should you say this as though you were using a knife to cut away your shackles, to blaze a straight path for yourself, you are falsifying to yourself, and he who speaks falsity has no power at all.

When you say, "I am perfect; I am well," you are not saying this to free yourself, but you are saying this in *joyous recognition.* If you think, "Now, I must inject something into my statements of Truth if I wish to experience them, if I wish to bring them to pass; I must cultivate a loving attitude; I must put expectation into my mind; I must actually feel that by saying these statements of Truth and expecting good to come from them that good will come" — oh, no, this is not looking up. This not seeing "Jesus only."

Rather is it as though you were in the kitchen saying, "Now, I must make a cake, for we must have cake for supper. I will use so much sugar and flour. I must not forget the eggs and the baking powder, for my cake will not be good until I have all these items. Then I must stir and stir and stir, for it says in the book that in order to have a good cake one must beat and beat and beat. Now I will put it into the oven and wait, and perhaps, *perhaps*, it will turn out a good cake."

Dear friend, is this an illustration of the way you are demonstrating? Are you looking at your experience much the same as this — thinking of God and reality and healing as though you were preparing a meal? You are not to cultivate a love for Truth as though you were polishing a piece of furniture. Love must be a *living* thing, and we have this love already deep, deep in our hearts, and when we look there, it flares up into a living burning thing.

What care we about the words that we use in treatment? Whether we are sitting or standing or walking? We are with our God, and we do not say,

"I must repeat it this way," or, "I must add this or that," but we forget all as we look upon Truth. We forget all except, "There is now no condemnation." We know that we are in Christ Jesus, for His love is in our hearts, and did not He say this would be where we would always find Him? And His name is in our foreheads, and His will is our Intelligence, and His way is the way of our being.

Now, when our hearts are alive and aflame with love, what do we care for details? What do we care how we give a treatment? *It is what is in our hearts that counts*, is it not? Even in our everyday life we can experience this freedom as though we did not have to measure and weigh and count.

I recall one day that after I had made a cake and placed it in the oven (filled all the time with thoughts far away from cake making), another in the kitchen exclaimed, "You forgot to put in the baking powder!" I laughed in sheer abandon. "Well, what if I did? I don't care. It will be the best cake I ever made. Pooh, what has a cake to say about how it shall be."

And at that moment it seemed just that way to me. Later that cake was pronounced a great success. It is wonderful to carry this feeling, "There is no condemnation," for one then walks in a world of enchantment and beauty.

Now, you do not have to put anything into the Word that you speak to make it true, to make it externalize. *It is already there!* All that you would put into it is there already. Oh, if we could always know this! Everything is in the Word, even before we speak it! We do not speak Truth thereby to bring It out into manifestation, but we speak It knowing It is true. We say It in glad recognition of Its ever-present reality. We say It as announcement, acknowledgment.

The reality of the Word is I AM. The Word is Christ, Truth, I AM THAT I AM. There is no condemnation now to rest upon you. You are to understand that what you call your wrong thinking has no power to hold or to bind you, for you are free in Jesus Christ. You are to know yourself a perfect being, an infinite, immortal being. This is freedom, emancipation, deliverance, insight.

Said a wonderful teacher of high mysticism, "There is a miracle-working Presence. It is man's privilege to make identification with the miracle-working Presence till he himself is a miracle-working presence, spilling over with new radiations as the opened flower spills over with new perfumes. ... It is from gaze toward one, victorious, indestructible Minister of the Almighty Original ever standing in our midst, saying, 'Lo, I am with you alway,' that we catch the keynote to victorious ministry....

"'In a very little while Lebanon shall be a fruitful field.' ... Lebanon stands for the Soul type, the Jesus Christ standard, Strong Son of God, Everlasting Friend, always with us, asking only recognition by praiseful description to be promptly fruitful after His own pattern, till earth's cities and plains are filled with men fulfilling untellable triumphs. ... Choose to set the inner eye toward the prize of the Lord Christ's healing face looking toward us—Strength of the nations, joy of the world" (Emma Curtis Hopkins).

The perfect practice or religion is not the following of a certain creed, not the repetition of certain words or formulas, not the attendance at certain churches. Religion is something much *deeper* than this, much *nearer* to us than this. It is that warmth of feeling, that thrill of the heart which cannot be put into words. Religion is that which satisfies the hunger and quenches the thirst for righteousness, right understanding.

Religion is the Spirit that maketh alive! Religion is the river of the water of life! It is said that when one comes into this understanding, one knows, because He Himself is this understanding.

"There is therefore now no condemnation for those who are in Christ Jesus."

Chapter VI

REFLECTION

If the discovery of a mental universe leads one into the belief that the mental world is real, then of what advantage to him is this discovery?

How can he consistently declare the unreality of sickness and evil and at the same time believe that sickness is mental, for if the mind be reality, then the sickness must be reality also. Thus confusion and disaster set in for one who holds to the reality of mind and the unreality of evil.

When one says that what is called disease, sin, and death are appearance only, of what advantage is this, and how will this announcement redeem the world? But if one traces a condition back farther than the mind, then he has a science which is beyond the mind, has he not?

To make a reality out of the mind and out of mental creation is to gain nothing by the knowledge that all is mind, but to reach up and beyond the mind and beyond mental creation into Intelligence, one has a science that understands Intelligence and Its perfect reflection.

Health, goodness, love, harmony are not made by thinking. They are not thought creations. *They are realities*, independent of all that one may think, whether right or wrong. No matter what anyone may think is wrong about him, such wrong thinking cannot interfere with his actual being, for at that very moment he is a perfect being without spot or blemish. And no matter what good thoughts one may be holding, neither do these good thoughts make him any different from what he is; therefore, it is truly announced that thought is not power.

Truth is all the power there is, and Truth is above mind and above appearance and above thinking.

Now, how many, leaping into the belief that all is mind and resting right here, have found a mental devil in this realm? How many, in losing the material realm or belief in matter and consequently losing a personal devil, nevertheless have found a devil of greater skill and power in this new realm of mind which is entered?

Is it not sad that such a state of ignorance should be entertained, that is, the belief in animal magnetism, the mental devil of the mental world?

Hearts have broken, families have been separated, difficulties that could not be named have arisen because of this new devil which, being in the mind, is believed to be ever-present. The terror, the fear, the agony that has sprung from belief in animal magnetism has far outstripped the fear and struggle for him who believed in a personal devil.

To be taught that thoughts are things; that thought is power; that unless one guards himself day and night through denial, at any moment evil thoughts from others may come into his mind, taking possession of his feeling to the extent that sickness results in his body and perhaps touches his dear ones and his business and environment is to be taught a falsity.

It is time the world wakens to the understanding that the only Mind there is, is the Mind of Intelligence, that any other mind is nothing and can do nothing.

With the devils of mortal mind, error, malicious animal magnetism, Roman Catholicism, what a lion's den there is before one! Is it any wonder that he trembles and fears and lives his daily life in struggle and terror?

Those who have plunged into *mental* sickness, *mental* difficulties, *mental* evil, and *mental* devils have but jumped from the pan into the flame. Now, this state of affairs has risen simply because it has not been discovered or made plain to one that in reducing evil to mind, he has at that moment reduced it to nothingness. It is time one knew true emancipation and what this includes, for to fear your own fear and to think of your brother man as holding thoughts that will injure you is grave ignorance.

Why has all this ignorant state of fearing animal magnetism and Roman Catholicism come into existence? Why has it been thought and taught in one breath that God is love and in another breath that one should work for protection daily against all forms and names of evil? Does it seem consistent, does it seem like a religion of love and understanding to place God on one side and a list of mental devils on the other side and to believe that each day you must take these mental devils up one by one and "handle them," taking out their sting, until the next day when you repeat the process? Does this sound like a science of Intelligence?

Let us look at this matter long enough so that we gain a very clear understanding, and let us see if we can see more plainly than ever before the temple or science of Truth as it is.

When the statement is thrown out to the world, "All is mind," just what does this mean? What does the word *all* include? Does it mean that all good is mind, or does it mean that all evil is mind, or does it mean that everything, both good and evil, is mind? Unless one knows and intelligently understands this tremendous point, how is he able to proceed? And is it not because one has not clearly understood the meaning of this statement that fear, confusion, discord, and strife shake the field today?

We will now start our premise upon Truth, God, Reality, heaven, wholeness, completeness, I AM THAT I AM, and ask, "Is this mental? Is this the "all" that is mental? Is God, Truth, I AM, mental?" Most certainly not. Truth is not mental. The starting point of Truth is not the mind. The definition of *mental* is "pertaining to the mind" —the human mind, called the mentality. Now, you can readily see that Truth is higher than the mind or mentality and that, therefore, Truth is not mind, and Truth is not mental.

Goodness, joy, praise, harmony, peace are not mental states, but they belong to Reality. They are not the product of the mind; they are not creations, but they are one with Truth, Reality, without beginning or end. They are inherent in being —in *your* being. Therefore, we repeat: health, sinlessness, peace, glory are not created states of mind, but are qualities of Soul, of Intelligence, Self, and are thus *self-existent realities.*

When it is stated, "All is mind," this declaration does not apply to Reality. Then what does the *all* mean? I will tell you. *It means creation.* All creation is mental. Had the word been given out, *All creation is mental, hence is not reality,* this would have cleared away much strife and struggle.

171

All that springs from the mind is mental. This does not mean that such creation is evil, but it means that a mental creation is something that is begun, started, and will therefore have an end. We have heard that someday the world will come to an end. Well, it is true that as one beholds the Promised Land his world of mental creation comes to an end.

Anything that is begun is not Truth or Reality and so has a limited number of days. Mental creation has been termed by some teachers a "counterfeit creation." At any rate, mental creation is not the perfect world. When you look around and see what is called evil, sin, sickness, poverty, and death, this is a mental creation; this had a beginning and will have an ending, for it is not Truth.

Truth is *all there is,* and besides Truth there is nothing else. Then all that is mind and all that is created through mind must be recognized as nothing, as illusion, hence, unreal, untrue.

You cannot have Truth and have something else besides, for Truth is *all* there is. As before explained, the perfect world is not a creation, for the perfect world was never begun; it coexists with Truth. The perfect world is the perfect, changeless, eternal reflection of Truth and is the heaven which Jesus said is "at hand."

Now, to declare that fear is mental, that animal magnetism is mental; to have this vision and rest here in such belief; to say that sin, sickness and death are mental and are to be denied is like setting to work to build with your own hands a prison in which you shall live. The vision must now expand. Higher must the face be lifted to the Sun of Righteousness so that one may behold the greater view, the clinching point, which is: *all mental creation is nothing.*

The feet now feel the Rock beneath them. The eyes have the glow of peace and glory, and one knows that he has spoken the Word, "I am Truth, and besides Me there is none else!"

It is the understanding of this word *nothing* that crumbles the prison walls, breaks the yoke from off the neck, and tears away the veil of ignorance so that one says, "I am free!" What can equal the wonderful message of the allness of Truth, the presence now and here of heaven, the immortality and infinity of man, and the nothingness of all mental creation!

Instead of holding in your hand a long list of ugly names headed with "animal magnetism," now, with joy unspeakable, take that list and, using the intelligence of insight, write one word across it— the word *nothing.*

173

Just contemplate for a moment the difference between mere mental denial and insight, so that you do not walk in the dark but clearly see and understand. With mental denial one takes up a word, say, *malicious evil suggestions,* and declares, "I deny this. It has no power over me. It is not of God, and I am not afraid of it," yet all the time he is inwardly shuddering with unknown fear, as though he had a reptile in his hands, and is glad to place this mental devil back in the list to proceed with another.

Has it not occurred to you who do this that in putting back mental devils today and taking them up tomorrow you have brought them to life again? Each day you deny them you are making them more real to yourself, and then when you are told that your thinking gives a thing all the power it has over you, and you are unable to stop your fearful thinking—is this not enough of hell? What greater devil, what greater hell could one entertain than to feel that he is responsible for his fear and his trouble and yet be entirely unable to stop his thinking, which he is told is causing it?

Think of the joy, the freedom, the emancipation when one can look at the seeming snake in the rope and can know that it is nothing. And when one can perceive that the evil in the world is like the snake, nothing—is not this true liberation? The snake is mental, a mental creation, and all denial in the universe will not kill or destroy it; likewise all sin, sickness, death are mental creations, and all denials in the world will not destroy them.

Evil can never be destroyed by mere mental denial. Animal magnetism, fear, and all mental devils will continue to assume a presence as long as one sees them as something to be denied.

Insight is a quality of Intelligence. Denial seeks to destroy by tearing down, by overthrowing. Insight looks into, looks through, looks beyond and is the flash of light that *knows;* is the blaze of Intelligence that announces: *It is!* and *It is not!* It arrives without any process.

One does not deny the evil which he admits is present, but one denies that any evil is present. This point should be clear to you.

Fear springs from the mind and is thus a mental creation and for this very reason is nothing and can do nothing. Belief that evil can travel from one mind to another is pure delusion, for mind is nothing and belief is nothing. Just as long as you call fear a "belief" are you making it something, and as long as you name evil "appearance," you are assuming it a something to be destroyed. Let the mental devils be seen and recognized as *deceptions* because of the blur in our own eyes, for were we viewing the world of reality as it is, we would see nothing but harmony.

There is no way to take up evil suggestions and handle them, for how can you handle that which is nothing? Can you take the bear out of the pile of dirt and handle it? Can you see that as long as you admit that there is something to do, a something to deny, a something to destroy, just so long are you admitting the presence of something besides Truth, and in handling evil this way you but strengthen your fear in it?

> The one thing to do is to "know the Truth," which is that we are immortal beings in heaven now, and all mental creation is like a dream, is nothing.

We are Intelligence, and the world in which we are now living is the true world of reality. As the blur goes from our eyes, we see clearly that this is so. Insight is the open door; insight is the path which leads unto the perfect day, the day of divine illumination.

Spirit is not a mental realization. Spirit is not the way you think, nor is it any mental conviction that you may attain. Spirit is that which *is*. Spirit is the fact of man's perfection now. Should you say, "I have a pain in my body, and I am suffering with disease," Spirit is the fact that there is no such idea present in your mind; that there is no such thing in the objective world or in the subjective world.

Spirit is the fact that there is but one Man, but one Presence, but one All, but one Intelligence, but one world. Spirit is the fact that in the perfect world, the City of Glory, which fills all space and is all there is, there is but the victorious Christ which we are; that all men are this one Presence, now seeing, knowing, and reflecting harmony, love, health, abundance, and *no man is seeing or feeling anything other than this reality, for,* "I am Truth, and besides Me there is nothing else."

Many early scientists performed miracles as great as some recorded in the Bible, and they did so by letting the Spirit bear witness, that is, by putting the objective world of unreality and the subjective world of unreality entirely aside, knowing their nothingness or dream-like existence, and having the perception, the discernment of Spirit as all there is and all reflection as perfect and as eternal and as everlasting and as indestructible and as unchangeable as Spirit.

"He sent his word and healed them." This does not mean that he sent out of his mind a thought of health or healing, but it means that he sent the Word, *the living Truth,* the Spirit. He sent the Word that man is perfect with no need of changing, no need of healing, for *man is health!*

The Word of Truth is Truth, while a thought of Truth, springing from the mentality, is one's idea or opinion of Truth. The Word of Truth blazes through the mind, piercing it; thus, it has been truly said that mind reflects Truth. The mentality does not originate Truth through its conscious thinking operation, but Truth is reflected by the mind. We are never the mind or the mentality. We are Intelligence.

For all troubles and evils, one has the same medicine—Truth, Spirit, the Word—and the Word is:

> Man is unborn, immortal, eternal, unchangeable being, living now in the perfect, heavenly City. There is no condemnation over me. There is no one seeing me other than what I am. There is one Presence, Power, Intelligence, Word, and I am this, for this is *all there is,* and there is nothing else for man to be. There is no prison; there is no lack; there is no loss; there is no condemnation in all the universe of God. There is only Love divine, filling every breast, lighting every heart with living flame.

This treatment is an acknowledgment of Truth. This treatment is the Word. This treatment is the Spirit, or the fact—that which is.

In the science of Omnipotence, one does not think that he must have the patient before him as he delivers healing to him. He does not think, "Now if I am to heal the sick, cast out devils, raise the dead, I must have my tools at hand; I must use them correctly if I am to obtain the right result." He does not say, as one confronted with a mathematical problem, "Now, there is a certain method to follow; there are certain steps I must take. I must watch closely; I must follow accurately if I am to attain the right result."

Such ideas should be swept out of the mind, for in trying to make Truth *true,* you are trying to add to Truth, and this cannot be accomplished. There is no process. There is no method. That which is true, is true *before* you give a treatment. That which is true is *all* there is.

Treatment is not the repetition of some supposedly correct statements. It is not the getting ready of the tools, or the sticks, but *treatment is the Word Itself,* is the living fire. To be sure, you will use right thoughts and you will think right thoughts, yet these thoughts are not the fire, for the Spirit only is the blaze of Light, "which lighteth every man that cometh into the world." Intelligence is in You, Self. You, Self, are Intelligence, and your mind, like a mirror, reflects this Intelligence and delivers It as right thinking.

Many ask their teacher, "Why am I not healed? I have been faithful to the reading and studying, faithful to the declarations and denials, but the healing does not come."

The laying on of the sticks, the getting ready of the fire is not enough; one must have the ignition, the knowing, the accepting, the full believing that omnipotent good is here and is *all there is,* that there is no other power or presence. One must know this, not with his mind or intellect, but with his *heart,* with his love, for the heart is where the fire burns, and the knowing with the heart, blazing of the heart, is the Light of Truth which is the cancellation of anything unlike itself.

> As the light takes up the shadow because of its nothingness, so Truth takes up what is called sin, disease, and evil in the same way.

This spark within you—the light that lighteth every man—must flame up, must leap into living being. It is rightly called the consuming fire, bursting the seeming veil of ignorance and delivering before your very eyes the perfect health, the perfect world— Yourself as you are.

The story of the lion cub brought up in the belief that he was a sheep, I related in former work, but it is so clearly illustrative of one's being what he is that it will bear repetition.

It seems, so the story runs, that a baby lion escaped from its fond mother and wandered off by itself into the open fields. Now, it chanced at that time that a mother sheep was grieving because of the loss of her baby lamb, and when she espied the baby lion, her mothering heart took him at once and cared for him as she would her very own.

So the cub grew and thrived under the belief that he was a sheep. He took on the traits and manners of his foster mother in her shyness and gentleness, even to her fear of dogs.

One day there chanced to come that way a lion of wisdom, a great male beast who took in at a glance the situation before him, how the cub was deceived so that he had forgotten his real being and now thought himself other than what he was; and this majestic creature decided that this cub should know the truth.

Calling the frightened cub-sheep aside, he told him the truth about himself, that he was not a sheep, that he was a lion like himself, but the cub was unbelieving. Then the great lion led the cub-sheep away to a lake, whose quiet surface was like crystal, and he forced him to look into the lake where could plainly be seen their reflections, the cub manifesting the same being as the great lion at his side, but even then he would not understand. He thought himself a sheep, and blinded by his ignorance, though he saw his own reflection like the lion at his side, even then he would not believe.

Now the great beast of the forest was incensed, infuriated at such willful ignorance that there could be such a thing as a creature who would not know himself as he is, who would believe himself a meek, fearful sheep instead of the mighty king of beasts, and he gave vent to his wrath in a great roar that fairly shook the earth and which reverberated far and near.

Then it was that the fire ignited in the heart of the cub. The spark blazed up within him as he *listened to his own language,* and with this burst of light, with this flame of fire, out of him came the answering call—*the roar of a lion.* Then he knew. Then he understood his real being, and with the courage born of a lion, he dashed off to the great forest beyond.

Thus it is with us. The fire must be kindled within the heart; it must flame until it pierces the cloud of nothingness, and then that in us will answer back the true language, "I Am, *I can, I will.*"

While man thinks himself other than what he is, thinks himself sick and poor and sad, he is under a delusion. He has, in his dream, wandered away from his home and forgotten his real being. The victorious Jesus announced to such, "I am the door," and entering this door, man finds his real being, finds that he is not poor or deluded or sinful but that he is like unto the Son of God!

In the lesson of the cub-sheep, he was not changed from a lion into a sheep and then restored into his real being again. He was never at any moment other than a lion. His belief did not change his being; his thinking so did not make it so; he did not have to lose his sheep nature, nor did he have to destroy it or think it away. *It never was!*

Thus, in the discernment of Truth, in the science of Intelligence, the delusions or evils are not burned away or destroyed or changed as though they were something, but through the Intelligence which one *is*, they are found to be non-existent.

"Show us the Father," they insisted. "Tell us plainly who you are and what are we," and He answered, "He that seeth Me seeth the Father, and all shall know that I am in you, and you are in Me, and we are one and the same Being."

There is a door to heaven, and this door is *Jesus Christ*. "I am the door." As we look through this door, we see things as they are. To attempt to understand and teach the highest practice, the science of Truth, and not place the vision on the door that lights the heavenly City is to see through ignorance.

In my book *The Finished Kingdom*, the vision is placed toward the City Beautiful, the Perfect Land, that one may see where he walks, that one may

In His Name

know that the white fields are at hand and the Land of Promise is within our reach.

In the book *The Christ Within,* the second of the series, is shown the door, Jesus Christ, that one, after seeing the kingdom at hand, may enter through the door into its enjoyment. To understand Jesus Christ—to know who He was and why He came on earth and what relation he is to us—is to "Enter through the narrow gate."

In this present volume, the last of the series, the vision includes the finished kingdom and the victorious Jesus Christ, the I AM, and points out the highest practice. *This is the ministry of Truth.*

When one looks through the eyes of Love, he sees things as they are; he has the single eye, the eye of discernment, the vision of Truth. Love is that which melts the heart, that tears away the seeming veil, that pierces the cloud of nothing and delivers healing. And Truth is Love. How often do we hear it said, "It is the way you look at a thing that counts."

There is a story told in the East of a king who had no son to whom he might leave his kingdom, his power, and his dominion. It came to him one day that he would adopt a son, one whom he could consider his very own, a boy that would be all that his heart could desire, and so he called his trusty minister and told him to go out into the world and find such a son for him, find the boy that would delight his heart and his mind, that would be just what his own boy would be had he been granted his desire to be a father.

The minister went out and searched far and wide for such a boy, but always there was something lacking, for there was so very much to be desired; the lad must have so many accomplishments, must in every way appear suitable to grace such a throne. Finally, he gave up in despair, for he could find no such perfect child, and returning home, he told his wife all about his trip and its mission and his failure. Her eyes lighted with inner joy as she exclaimed, "Why, you should have told me before, and you would have saved yourself such failure. Come with me."

She took him into the adjoining room where stood their own small son, whom she proudly put into her husband's arms. "Why, of course," cried the man, "Here is the perfect child for the king. Why did I not think this before?" Then they dressed the child in his most suitable clothes, and proudly the minister took his own son to his king.

Now, when the child was presented to the king, who was all anticipation and longing, the king could not control his great disappointment and his scorn, for how could such a child be considered a son of his? This dark-skinned, ignorant-looking urchin to be king! He laughed the idea to scorn, while the father stood by unbelieving; for how could the king see this child homely and ignorant and undesirable, while he saw the child so beautiful and lovely and attractive?

When the king turned to him, asking how he could ever dream of such a thing as that this queer-looking child could be adopted as his own son, the minister answered, "Oh, King, could you only see what I see, you would see a most beautiful boy, lovely in every way. Could you but see the child as I see him, you would love him and would want him for your very own."

It is the door through which one looks that tells the story. It is the eye of Love that sees things lovely and divine. Looking through the eyes of wisdom and intelligence, the great lion knew the truth about the cub-sheep; looking through the eyes of love, the father saw the perfect child, fit for a king; and looking through the eyes of perfection, Jesus, the beloved, saw perfect beings and told them of their perfection in a perfect world.

Let us consider if we are looking through the eyes of Love, the eyes of Truth, seeing things as they are known by Truth, or if we are beholding things other than what they are because of the veil over our eyes, because of the blur in our vision.

In speaking of the removal of evil, sin, disease, and death, it is the same as saying that evil does not exist as a reality, for since it can be removed from experience, it is therefore unreality, nothing; for that which is something, that which is real, is changeless and cannot be moved.

Now, when we speak of Truth as removing evil or as healing disease, we understand that the removal of evil does not effect any change; the healing by Truth does not mean the actual healing of anything at all, for the body is not changed, the mind is not changed, the individual is not changed.

We say that Truth heals, and it is wonderful to be able to clearly and intelligently understand just what such a statement means. Simple illustrations best explain the seeming mystery. When you dream of seeing a large city, of visiting friends, entering stores and shops and viewing sights of interest and delight, where does this city go when you waken? Where are the shops and the friends when you waken from your dream?

You lose them, of course, but can you see that they were not actual and that in losing them they went without anything taking place? The same as on the moving-picture screen—changes are constantly taking place, people coming and going; still, nothing is actually happening, for there are no people there. There is nothing present but the white screen.

Also, when the form moves out of the mirror, it goes without going, for in such action as the moving of the reflection from the mirror, nothing is taking place; the mirror remains untouched, unchanged. Thus, it can be intelligently understood that a reflection is nothing; a picture is nothing, whether on the screen, in the mirror, or in the body. A reflection acts without acting and disappears without anything going away. The picture of disease in the body is the same as the picturization of form and action on the screen, in the dream, or in the mirror. If you can understand one, you can understand all.

Speaking of the picture which we have seen on the screen, we say, "He walked miles and miles over dry, sandy plains," yet we know all the time that the man whom we saw on the screen performing this act was only a picture. No man was present, no action was taking place, for a reflection or picturization is nothing in and of itself.

In the science of intelligent discernment, we reserve the same right of speech, the same understanding of affairs, when we say, "The swelling went down and entirely disappeared." We speak these words, yet we clearly understand that nothing whatever took place, any more than when the man walked across the plains or when we entered the store and shopped in our dream. We now understand that such action is no action, and in the disappearance of disease nothing has taken place.

The disease shown forth on the body is the picturization or reflection of wrong belief in the mind, and such picturization is nothing — the wrong thoughts are nothing; the mind itself is nothing.

The perfect, radiant Body, the Mind of Intelligence, the Being which is Truth is all there is, and nothing can be added to It or subtracted from It.

In the coming, enduring, disappearing of the dream, nothing has taken place. The man on the couch does not leave his room when he dines with his friends in another country, and it is true, as one teacher wrote in her textbook, "Undisturbed amid the jarring testimony of the material senses, Science ... is unfolding to mortals the immutable, harmonious, divine Principle — Life and the universe, ever-present and eternal" (Mary Baker Eddy).

A disease can no more get into the body than a flower can get into the mirror.

When one clearly understands that the picturization of disease in the body is merely a *reflection*, that the body acts like a mirror, reflecting the beliefs in the mind, one then loses his fear, for he can readily see that such reflection is nothing, and refusing to believe in the reality of disease, he now looks through it and beyond it, intelligently perceiving the nothingness of reflection, the nothingness of shadow, the nothingness of picturization.

If one does not believe in the reality of disease or fear it, it cannot remain. One does not dream of dining with kings while he is awake, yet in his sleep he may do so; but as soon as he wakens, the dream vanishes. So while one sleeps in the dream of material and mental existence, believing in the reality, the power, the actual presence in the body of disease and disorder, he has the experience of entertaining them; but as he wakens to the fact that he is a perfect, immortal, divine being in heaven, such conditions vanish.

"Ye shall know the truth, and the truth shall make you free." To understand the truth about evil and disease, which truth is to perceive their nothingness, is to be free from the dream. *Nothing from the external world is being reflected in the body; the picture is always thrown from within.* This then simplifies the treatment, for one knows where to meet the enemy. One knows that he must simply understand that wrong belief—belief in sickness, sin, and death—is nothing, has no presence, no power, no action.

To perceive this is to be lifted on high, and to be lifted on high is to deliver healing, power, strength, beauty, glory to yourself and to your world.

Goodness, health, harmony are not opposites of evil, disease, and discord. It is not Science to say that ignorance is the opposite of Intelligence. Health, harmony, intelligence—being *all* there is—*have no opposites*, and that which appears as an opposite is that which is but a picture, or nothing.

There is nothing which can oppose Truth. Why is this? Because the Truth is *all* there is. Evil has no presence, no power, no substance; it occupies no space, no position. Health, harmony, love is the true substance.

The power that annihilates disease is the discernment that Truth is omnipotent, omnipresent, and omniscient, and any appearance that does not testify to the allness, the ever-presence, the changelessness of health and harmony is the nature of a dream, a lie, a picture, and so is not anything at all.

Bullets fly and battles rage on the screen, yet when war is over, not even a hole is found in the white sheet. Is not this a marvelous illustration? The water, the fire, the torpedoes never touch the screen that they play upon. Let this tell you plainly that the disease, the pain, the swelling that you see manifested in the body *have never once touched the body.*

The body is as perfect now, as radiant and wonderful now, as before what you called disease and pain were reflected upon it. This understanding makes one feel as though a great load were lifted from him, and he feels power, strength, courage, as he sees clearly that the body needs no healing whatever, *that a picture or reflection of disease can move from the body as easily as a form can move from the picture screen or from the mirror.*

Now that you see through the deception of disease, you understand that healing by Truth is as though nothing were done in the objective world—the body—nor in the subjective world—the mentality. There is but the intelligent perception of Soul, which is the flash of light—removing, annihilating, absorbing the darkness of nothingness.

When a false creation disappears and the true reflection is again seen, this is called a miracle or a healing. So when one speaks of being healed of a certain disease, it should mean the same to you as though he were relating his dream of the night before.

In divine Mind, Intelligence, are the divine prototypes, images of Truth, which, like Truth, are perfect, changeless, constant, ever-present, infinite, and eternal.

As the idea *two* or *four* cannot be lost or sick or separated or destroyed, neither can the concept of the perfect body be other than like Truth which conceives it. Would it not be a queer thing if, while we are computing a mathematical sum, we should suddenly discover that there were no 6 available? We simply cannot imagine such a thing as a number being sick or meeting with an accident or being operated upon for disease. Such an idea is inconceivable, is it not?

Yet one may believe that an eye can be destroyed or a finger can be lost or a stomach can be sick. Now, if the idea *six* is above injury, disaster, sickness, and death, then how much more should the divine idea or image *finger* and *stomach* and *eye*, and all the concepts that go to make up the perfect body!

All the operations and diseases in the universe never touched the perfect concept of sight or hearing, of lungs or heart, of hand or foot. These are not ideas of mind, but are concepts of Intelligence, divine Mind, I AM, and are above birth, sickness, and destruction.

As there is no private 2 or 3, neither is there a private hand or foot. The concepts or divine prototypes are infinite, universal, beyond matter and beyond mind, "eternal in the heavens."

Truth is not that which changes us from physical beings into immortals, but Truth is that which shows us our real being to be like unto itself. "Grace and truth came by Jesus Christ." Jesus Christ as Emmanuel brought to immortals the message of liberty, freedom, harmony, the

In His Name

message of the transcendental, transdimensional City Beautiful, at hand, and the wonderful Kingdom of true, perfect, and divine images or ideas within.

Since I AM is above and beyond change, birth, evil, death, *so are also Its divine prototypes, ideals, images, concepts, and so are also their reflections or projections.* In order that one behold his reflection in the mirror, he places himself before the mirror, does he not? Then in the mirror he sees what is termed his reflection, which corresponds exactly to the form before it.

One might say that it takes light and also the presence of something before the mirror in order to have a reflection, and one might ask what it takes that one have the perfect projection or reflection of harmony and perfection in the body and in affairs. The answer is that Mind, *conscious of Its perfect concepts or divine ideas,* projects them or reflects them.

If one feels a pain in his finger, why would he deny the presence of pain yet not deny the finger? Because finger is a divine concept in Mind, Consciousness, and is universal, omnipresent, infinite, changeless, and eternal. Pain is an idea in the mentality. The idea, pain, is false, illusion.

Since there are no concepts of pain and disease in Consciousness, I AM, there can be no such reflections in the body. If you look into a mirror and see yourself very, very tall and thin, you know that this is a distortion, illusion; so if you look in your body and see pain and disease, this is a distortion, illusion. If you have pain instead of harmony, it is not that Mind is conscious of a concept *pain*, but it is that your mind is reflecting perfect ideas in a distorted fashion, the same as a mirror that is covered with dust will not act as a perfect reflector. So mind, believing in sin, disease, and evil, fails to image forth the true and perfect conception and ideas in Consciousness.

One may have the idea that a wall is solid and has resistance and that he must pass over it or around it if he wishes to be on the other side, that is, to one the wall is solid and resistant. To the illumined, the wall is like a mist, and he passes through it as though it were an open space. This does not mean that the wall is not there, but it means that to the consciousness of the illumined the hardness and the resistance are not there. Jesus proved this frequently. The walls were not solid and resistant to Him.

In my book *The Finished Kingdom*, I related my experience of passing through a horse and wagon. As many have written me for further explanation of this experience, I will say that it seemed to me exactly as though I were passing through a cloud. There was no solidity, no resistance. Many have asked, "What happened to the man and the horse

and wagon?" I cannot say. His experience, no doubt,
was quite different from mine. This is clearly
explained in a certain textbook of metaphysics:

"The heavens and earth to one human
consciousness ... are spiritual, while to another,
the unillumined human mind, the vision is
material. This shows unmistakably that what the
human mind terms matter and spirit indicates
states and stages of consciousness" (Mary Baker
Eddy).

My experience certainly delivered no harm to
the man. This brings to my mind an article which I
read in a newspaper many years ago. It told of a
man whose duty it was to deliver large sums of
money to a bank certain days in the week. This man
was a Christian Scientist. Now, it was pointed out
to him that a certain street which he must travel in
order to reach the bank was noted for its "hold-
ups" and he should therefore carry a firearm for
protection. This man considered the matter but
thought best to take Truth instead.

One day while on this street, he noted a rough-
looking man approaching and at once called upon
Truth and the promise, "I will be with thee in
trouble. I will not fail thee nor forsake thee." The
man passed by.

The very next day he saw this man's picture in
the paper and an account of his capture because of

some past offense. The Scientist went to this man in the prison and asked him if he had not intended to stop him the day before, and the man replied, "Yes, I had intended to rob you, but I would have been a fool to stop you when you had a man on both sides of you."

The Scientist had been alone, yet this man had seen "a man on both sides."

Does not this bring to your mind the scriptural account of Elisha? His servant came rushing to him with the news that a great army was coming toward them to fight them and cried, "Alas, my master! What shall we do?" And Elisha prayed that *the eyes of his servant might be opened,* and when the young man servant looked around him again, he saw that the mountain was full of horses and chariots!

Thus it is clearly shown that *what* we see is a matter of consciousness, or inner vision. The spiritual world is the world of perfect concepts, divine ideas, and as we place our vision here do we see and experience their presence. We place our vision on the risen, ever-present, never-absent Christ; we praise the free Spirit which knows beyond the mind; we know that, "If thine eye seek the Lord only, thy whole body shall be full of wisdom."

The High and Lofty One inhabiting Eternity cannot look upon evil, but beholds only the brightness of His own glory.

Chapter VII

HEALING MINISTRY

The supreme miracle is to discern the nothingness of both matter and mind and behold the allness of perfect man in the spiritual world now.

The virtue of a treatment is its flash of light, its glow of illumination, its spark of insight. My treatment is the understanding that nothing is to be changed; nothing is to be added or subtracted. I speak Truth for the joy of it, for the glory of God. I speak the Word not because I lack but because I *have*. I speak the Word not because I expect but because I *have arrived.* I do not speak Truth to heal sick people or to enlighten ignorant people, but I speak and I write Truth that immortals may drink with me of the *living* water — *the river of the water of Life!*

The science of Spirit is the science of discernment, the science of insight. Truth is not a subjective power, not like a great wind that rushes into the mentality, sweeping its thoughts around from one place to another, arranging, arresting, marshaling its beliefs and ideas. Truth does not have to be put into operation so that one will see discord disappear. Truth is not an attacking power, like a mighty general going out to battle and to kill.

True Science is above war, above change, above strife, above seeing evil that is to be destroyed. While mental healing would produce health, the science of Intelligence knows the *omnipresence of wholeness*. While mental healing would educate the mind—would give power, might, glory, and dominion to the mind—*the science of Truth gives all power to Soul, to I Am, to Self.*

I am not servant to my body, nor am I servant to my mind. I do not speak with my mind, nor am I dependent upon my thoughts. *I speak the Word!* The Word proceeds not from my mentality, but the Word proceeds from I Am, Soul.

I acknowledge that the Word is Power, is Spirit, is Life, is God Almighty. I acknowledge there are no mistakes to be corrected; there is no body to be healed; there is no mind to be educated; there is no evil to be destroyed; there is no disease to be overcome. I acknowledge treatment is not a means to an end. I acknowledge Life, Truth, Love, Spirit, Self to be *One* and to be *All* and that there is nothing besides!

There is no life, truth, intelligence, substance in the body or in the mind. All is infinite Mind and Its infinite manifestation, *for God is all there is!* Spirit is immortal Truth! Spirit is the real and eternal! And man is like Spirit—birthless, ageless, deathless, all -glory, all-majesty, and all-splendor.

I do not rename evil, but I cast out of mind the deception called evil, *the belief that there is evil.* Understanding is not mental. I AM is Understanding. Mentality is not the seat of power, for mind without Intelligence back of it would be unable to know anything. I do not manipulate the mind by means of suggestions. The illumined message of Truth is that I am perfect being *now*— complete, whole— and the antidote for all seeming trouble is to discern its deception, hence, know its unreality, negation.

The Kingdom Message is that we are spiritual, perfect beings in heaven now!

The material vision is that man is material, mortal, made of dust. The mental vision is that man is a mental being living in a mental universe; that he must climb, he must unfold, he must surmount difficulties, he must overcome evil with the power and the might of his mind. The Kingdom Message, the spiritual, high vision, is that man is a spiritual, perfect, complete being in heaven now.

Thinking does not bring emancipation, liberation, deliverance. Insight alone beholds that which is to be *all* there is and that there is none else. Insight, illumination, discernment sweep into the mind, piercing it as though tearing off a veil, as though removing a blur and delivering the vision of the perfect universe at hand.

The snake in the rope is not to be destroyed by striking it with stones. The highest practice is not to attack evil, but to perceive the universe as it *is*, to see things as they *are*, to view that which is, *as it is!*

I am not to change body or mind, but I am to become aware of *changeless being*, of illumined Consciousness. I am to know that there is one Spirit, one Truth, one Consciousness, one Self, one I AM, and that this is *one whole* in which is no separation or division. I am to intelligently understand the *oneness* and *totality* of Life and Being.

One may think that if only he has set before him an intelligent explanation of evil he may then get at its root, get at its cause and thereby remove it, but evil is not to be removed by getting at its cause. *Evil, is to be removed by discerning that it is without cause!*

The bear in the pile of dirt is not removed by finding out from what direction it came. Two and two are five is not destroyed by discovering its origin. It is because there is no reason back of evil that you are unable to find the cause of its presence. You do not understand your dream while you are in the dream, but when you waken, you understand its nothingness.

Do not expect to find in the mind that which is not in the mind. To look for health, joy, and understanding in the mind is as foolish as to look for gold in the leaves of a tree or to look to a school for instruction which is not given in that school. You look for gold in its place; you look for stars in their place; and you look for Intelligence where it is to be found—in God, in I AM, in Soul.

By knowing the nothingness of nothing do we walk in the City of Righteousness, the finished Kingdom—do we waken in the perfect world, governed by a perfect Principle.

Treatment is to waken an individual so that he may behold himself as he is!

My thoughts are true and right thoughts, because they spring from Intelligence. My life is pure and perfect, because it springs from the fountain of the river of Life. My peace is all-satisfying, because it is established on high—because it is not dependent upon body or mind but is the peace of God. My health is fixed, constant, eternal, changeless, because it is the wholeness of I AM. Truth in the unseen is perfect, and Truth in Its image and reflection is perfect. The reflection is as changelessly perfect as are the divine concepts in divine Mind.

There is now no condemnation to rest upon me, for I am enlightened. I know the Truth. I know there is but *one* Presence, but *one* Self, and I am this. I am one with God. I am one with everlasting Life. I am one with wholeness. I am one with understanding. I am one with the beauty of Holiness.

The kingly Science, the Jesus Christ Message, the Word—*in His Name*—is, "Rise and walk! Go in peace, and nothing shall in any wise hurt you!"

Believe that you have now in the spiritual world, and you shall receive even in what you call the material and mental world, for there is no world except the world of reality, the world of heaven and harmony.

"Though thy sins be as crimson, they shall be white as snow." You cannot be other than who and what you are. You cannot change from your *changeless state*. There is no other man but the man of God, the man without spot or blemish, the glorious Spirit of God.

> *I* am Spirit. *I* am imperishable, unspoilable, sinless, changeless being. *I* am Intelligence, knowing the power, the radiance, the strength, the completion, the perfection of Myself .
>
> My body is the radiance of the perfect day, with face as the sun and with raiment as the light, without spot or blemish—the transcendent image of Truth.

This is the Truth that I must know! This is the river of the water of Life! This is the glory from on High! This is the finished Kingdom and the Christ within! This is the Word which I utter *in His name!*

FINIS

About the Author

Lillian DeWaters was born in 1883 and lived in Stamford, Connecticut. She grew up with a Christian Science background and in her early teens began to study metaphysics and on that same day to seriously study the Bible. "It was from the Bible that I learned to turn from all else to God direct .... What stood out to me above all else was the fact presented, that when they turned to God they received Light and Revelation; they walked and talked with God; and they found peace and freedom."

She published a few books while actively within the Christian Science organization, and then in 1924 she had an awakening experience when it was as though a veil was parted and Truth was revealed to her. From that point she began to receive numerous unfoldments which led to her separation from the Christian Science organization.

She created her own publishing company and wrote over 30 books published in 15 languages. She was known as a well-known teacher and healer known throughout the world.

All of her books were written based on her direct unfoldments of Absolute Truth.

Made in the USA
Columbia, SC
13 November 2020